MANIFESTATION THROUGH THE 12 LAWS OF THE UNIVERSE

MANIFEST YOUR DREAMS AND ATTRACT ABUNDANT
PEACE • MONEY • HAPPINESS • FREEDOM

BELLE MOTLEY

TABLE OF CONTENTS

INTRODUCTION

Everything you want is out there waiting for you to ask.
Everything you want also wants you. But you have to take
action to get it.

— JACK CANFIELD

Knowledge Is Not Enough

Welcome to an enlightening journey that will unlock your
inner power through the awe-inspiring Laws of the Universe.
This book unveils twelve magnificent Laws that govern everything from the smallest particles to the grandest galaxies,
weaving the fabric of our reality in ways we could never have
imagined. As you delve deeper into these principles, you'll

discover the intricate connections between your thoughts, emotions, actions, and the world around you.

You will uncover the keys to unlocking a life of abundance, joy, and fulfillment, learning how to harness these Universal forces to shape the world around you. With this newfound wisdom, the life you've always dreamed of is within your reach, waiting for you to embrace its infinite potential. This book will also provide you with practical exercises and techniques to help you apply these Laws effectively in your daily life.

But knowledge alone is not enough; it is through the application of these profound insights that you will truly experience their transformative power. This book will equip you with the understanding and tools necessary to ignite positive change and take control of your destiny. Along the way, you'll find inspiration from stories of individuals who have successfully harnessed the power of these Laws to create meaningful change in their lives.

Understanding and taking action can significantly enhance not only your own life but also contribute to a better world. In this era of apparent global turmoil, each of us must play a role in creating a more harmonious and sustainable planet for everyone. The time for change is now - we can make a difference, and it starts with changing your own life.

The Laws of the Universe Can Help You Succeed

You may be approaching this book feeling disheartened, as if the Universe is conspiring against you. Despite your best efforts, life's obstacles might seem insurmountable, and the path to your dreams clouded. However, within these pages lies the solace and wisdom you seek. You're not alone, nor are you defeated. Armed with the incredible power of the Laws of the Universe, which you're about to uncover, you will find the strength and strategies to surmount challenges and realize your most cherished aspirations.

Throughout this book, you'll explore the role each of these Laws plays in shaping your reality, as well as their interrelatedness and synergy. You'll learn how to leverage the power of these Laws to overcome setbacks, create new opportunities, and turn your dreams into realities. Moreover, you'll discover practical strategies for maintaining a positive mindset, cultivating resilience, and sustaining motivation as you work toward your goals.

You might have heard of the Laws of the Universe before but found them difficult to grasp. Fear not, for this book is designed to guide you through the mysteries without overwhelming you with complex terminology. By the time you reach the last page, you will possess a deep understanding of these principles and be equipped to harness their transformative potential.

I've Been in Your Shoes

No one is born with the innate knowledge of the Laws of the Universe. Like any skill, it must be learned and practiced to harness its power. My mission is to share my insights and experiences with you, guiding you toward a life of harmony, profound peace, healing, and purpose. This transformative journey has the potential to reshape your destiny, leading you down a path that resonates with your deepest values, passions, and beliefs, ultimately unveiling a sense of balance and fulfillment.

Having been through my own struggles, moments of feeling lost, and even lying on my deathbed, I can genuinely empathize with the challenges you may be facing. I am deeply committed to sharing the knowledge I've gained to empower others who may be experiencing similar hardships. Through the insights and experiences in this book, you'll discover a roadmap to a brighter, more joyful future.

My journey has equipped me with invaluable perspectives and tools that have revolutionized my life, bringing happiness, peace, and abundance. I am thrilled to share these transformative treasures with you and support you in forging your own path to success and fulfillment. Together, we can embrace the adventure ahead and create a future that truly shines as we learn and grow. Through the power of shared experiences, personal stories, and practical wisdom, we can support and inspire one another on this incredible journey toward self-discovery and personal growth.

Manifestation and The Twelve Laws

Manifestation refers to the tangible realization of a thought, idea, desire, or plan, which can be either positive or negative and may occur without conscious awareness. It encompasses anything that materializes in your life, be it a physical object, a feeling, an emotion, or any form of information (Sholer, 2017). Intentionally bringing an idea into existence also constitutes manifestation, involving the transformation of an abstract concept into a concrete reality. To achieve success in life, one can utilize manifestation techniques that tap into universal energy and focus on these Twelve Universal Laws:

1. Law of Divine Oneness
2. Law of Vibration
3. Law of Correspondence
4. Law of Attraction
5. Law of Inspired Action
6. Law of Perpetual Transmutation of Energy
7. Law of Cause and Effect
8. Law of Compensation
9. Law of Relativity
10. Law of Polarity
11. Law of Rhythm
12. Law of Gender

In the upcoming chapters, we will delve into the spiritual meaning of the Universe and then explain each Law of the Universe in detail. As you progress, you'll discover the Laws and how to incorporate them into your life to accomplish your desired outcomes. These Laws are essential in aiding you to connect with your higher self and better understand your true purpose. By recognizing that the Universe is conscious and willing to help you accomplish your objectives, you'll be able to explore your desires on a deeper level.

Alongside the exploration of each Law, you will find real-life examples, case studies, and practical exercises that will help you understand and apply these principles in your daily life. By actively engaging with these practices, you will gradually develop the skills and mindset necessary to manifest your dreams and aspirations, leveraging the incredible power of the Laws of the Universe to your advantage.

It is my heartfelt mission to guide you toward a life of profound purpose and fulfillment by sharing these powerful principles. I am deeply invested in your journey and am committed to helping you connect with your higher self and realize your true potential. The Universe is a conscious, benevolent force, ready and waiting to support you in achieving your goals. So, let us embark on this extraordinary adventure together and explore the boundless possibilities that await you. With the Laws of the Universe as your guide, prepare to be inspired, empowered, and forever transformed.

1

A COSMIC CONNECTION

As far as I can tell, it's just about letting the Universe know what you want and then working toward it while letting go of how it comes to pass.

— JIM CARREY

WE ARE ALL IN THIS TOGETHER

Many believe the Universe is not just a collection of inanimate objects but a higher being with its own consciousness. Different names may refer to the Universe, but all those names ultimately refer to the same entity. Some think of it as a divine force governing the world, while others consider it a living, breathing entity connected to all life on Earth.

From a spiritual perspective, the idea of the Universe is synonymous with a higher power. It is often referred to as God, Source, Consciousness, Spirit, Being, Higher Self, or even Love (Wong, 2021). Rely on your intuition to guide you toward a name that resonates with you. It is not the name that matters; rather, it is the belief that there is something greater than ourselves that exists.

Humans have sought a higher power throughout history by turning to different religions and spiritual practices. This deep-rooted desire to connect with a higher power transcends language, culture, and geographical boundaries. As a result, people from all over the world seek to connect with their higher powers in diverse and personal ways. Whether through prayer, meditation, or other forms of spiritual practice, we continue to explore the mysteries of the Universe in the hope of gaining a deeper understanding of ourselves and the world around us.

The Universe As Love

This all-pervading energy is often referred to as a never-ending stream of love, as it is believed that love is the ultimate high-frequency vibration that the Universe operates on (Wong, 2021). It is a fundamental life force that underpins everything and everyone, and it keeps flowing even when we are unaware of it. Whenever we choose to recognize and connect with this ever-flowing energy of love, we're able to tap into its boundless potential and experience a deep, soulful transformation. Being aligned with the Universe is all about syncing with its high vibrational energy of love. The Universe continuously responds to the energy we emit, which manifests in the form of people, situations, and experiences that match our vibrational frequency.

Authentic Spiritual Significance of the Universe

We are not just mere observers of the Universe's magnificence but active participants in its infinite possibilities. Every living and non-living thing represents a unique expression of the Universe's grandeur—an intricate piece of the cosmic puzzle. It is truly humbling to think that we have been bestowed with the privilege of co-creating this awesome phenomenon of the Universe.

Connecting to the Universe

The spiritual meaning of the Universe remains a mystery despite centuries of searching and theorizing. However, by studying its clues and patterns, we can make some progress and glimpse its infinite wisdom. One of the best interpretations of the meaning of the Universe is that it is all about connection. It is a vast, interconnected web of energy that brings everything and everyone within it together.

So, how do we connect with the Universe? To do so, we need to quiet our minds and open our hearts. By meditating on the nature of the Universe or simply spending time in nature, we can attune our energy to that of the Universe (Rotar, 2022). The Universe continuously responds to the energy we give off, and by sending out high-vibrational, positive energy, we will receive high-vibrational, positive results. In contrast, low vibrational and negative energy will yield low vibrational and negative results. Embracing the spiritual significance of the Universe means realizing that our actions have a profound impact not only on ourselves but also on the Universe itself.

WE ARE THE UNIVERSE

"It's like we've forgotten who we are… we used to look up in the sky and wonder at our place in the stars," says Joseph Cooper in Christopher Nolan's Interstellar (2015). Our connection with the Universe is of great importance when it comes to manifesting our dreams. Through this connection, we can attain the clarity, inspiration, and guidance needed to reach our aspirations.

Gazing At

The human fascination with gazing into the darkness above and contemplating our relationship with the wider cosmos has endured from ancient civilizations to modern times. As we look upwards, we focus our minds and intentions, seeking to understand not only the objective reality of the Universe but also our own unique connection to it. In this way, our curiosity leads us to our first conscious encounter with the Universe. From this initial meeting, we are forever changed, becoming part of the vast and intricate web of existence that we call the Universe.

Knowledge Of

As we observe the Universe, we seek answers to our most enduring questions. While we may not be able to comprehend its vastness completely, there are some parts we can understand. This understanding comes through naming and analyzing what we can see and attaching information to those names (Wang, 2016). By doing this, we are able to capture and remember the things we observe and, therefore claim to "know" something about the Universe.

Identifying With

The more we gaze at it and come to know about the Universe, the more we start identifying with it. According to Jom (2022), the structures of the Universe and the human brain are strikingly similar. The explosion of supernova stars formed various elements in the periodic table, some of which constitute the essential building blocks of the human body.

As we learn more about the Universe, we begin to form feelings about it and express them naturally. Our bodies are similar to other galactic matters, and some of our cultural products are similar to the products of nature (Wang, 2016). For example, just as a tree grows and changes over time, human cultures also evolve and change over time. Both are dynamic and constantly adapting to their environments.

Making Connections for Manifestation

All activities mentioned above have something in common—they are all ways to connect with the Universe (Wang, 2016). When we gaze at the night sky, we realize that we are not alone in the Universe and that the stars and planets we see are all part of the same cosmos. This realization develops a sense of belonging and understanding that empowers us and helps us feel less lonely and more fulfilled. By understanding this connection, we can harness the Universe's power to manifest our dreams and take responsibility for our thoughts and emotions. Manifestation enables us to access boundless energy and synchronize our existence with the interconnected network of energy that links all things together.

UNIVERSAL ENERGY AND MANIFESTATION

Manifestation is all about tapping into the energy surrounding us and using it to our advantage. As we have discussed, the Universe is a web of powerful energy that we are connected to. Individuals can harness that energy by intentionally communicating their desires and plan to the Universe. This involves using our thoughts, beliefs, emotions, and actions to create the reality we want to experience (Green, 2022). To manifest what it is we desire, we must be clear about what we want and focus our energy on achieving those goals.

What Is Universal Energy?

Energy is the fundamental building block of matter and is present all around us. It cannot be created or destroyed, as recognized by Albert Einstein, who pointed out the concept of shaping our own realities rooted in the laws of physics (Hurst, 2021). Understanding that everything is energy allows us to appreciate life's underlying forces and use that energy in our manifestations.

Transforming Reality

We must learn to use the energy at our disposal to make significant changes in our lives and the world around us. Katharine

Hurst (2021) suggests utilizing the brain's reticular activating system (RAC) by focusing on our desired outcomes, which can attract positivity or accelerate progress. Practicing mindfulness can also benefit our mental state by helping us become more self-aware and observant of our emotions and environment.

Manifestation Facts and Myths

Visualizing our goals and focusing on the necessary steps to achieve them is crucial for manifesting success. Positive visualization can bring many benefits, including improved coping skills and decreased depression. Studies such as Blankert and Hamstra's (2016) study on tennis players have shown the effectiveness of visualization techniques in achieving desired outcomes. The results showed that those who used positive visualization were more successful than those who did not.

However, manifestation requires more than just visualizing; we must also connect with our desires on an emotional level. **Immersing ourselves in the sensory experience of our desires and feeling emotions like love, happiness, appreciation, and gratitude can help align us with the vibration of abundance and attract positivity into our lives.** I have highlighted this, as our feelings are essential to our desired outcome. In addition, by engaging all our senses, we can activate our subconscious mind, which creates our reality.

It is important to understand that manifestation has limits, and certain things remain beyond our control. For example, in Blankert and Hamstra's research, tennis players didn't win every game after using positive visualization, but their overall performance improved. It's important to recognize that manifestation alone may not solve deeply rooted systemic issues, such as poverty and discrimination. While it can contribute positively, tackling these problems requires broader societal efforts. Furthermore, it's crucial to remember that focusing solely on the end goal without taking action may hinder progress.

Manifestation is not just making a wish; it's a skill that requires us to tap into our innermost feelings and recognize our ability to influence our mental experiences and actions. We can enhance our likelihood of success by believing in ourselves and our desires and experiencing them on a visceral level. If you can envision yourself as prosperous, truly believe in it, and feel it within your entire being, prosperity will follow.

Now, let's explore the concept of detachment and how it plays a vital role in the manifestation process.

Detachment

Detachment is a crucial element in the manifestation process because it allows you to maintain a positive and relaxed state of mind, which is essential for attracting positive experiences and outcomes. Here's how detachment relates to manifestation as a whole:

1. **Removes resistance:** Attachment to specific outcomes or the way things "should" happen can create resistance, making it difficult for the manifestation to occur. Detachment helps remove this resistance, allowing the manifestation to unfold more naturally.

2. **Reduces negative emotions:** Detachment enables you to release feelings of desperation, anxiety, and fear that may hinder the manifestation process. By letting go of these emotions, you create a more positive and receptive mindset conducive to manifesting your desires.

3. **Allows for divine timing:** By practicing detachment, you trust that the Universe knows the best timing for your manifestation. This trust enables you to be patient and open to receiving your desires at the right time rather than trying to force things to happen on your terms.

4. **Opens up possibilities:** When you detach from specific outcomes or methods, you allow the Universe to bring your desires to you in the best possible way. This openness can lead to unexpected opportunities and experiences that may not have been possible if you were attached to a particular path.

5. **Enhances trust in the Universe:** Detachment helps you develop trust in the Universe and its ability to provide for your needs. This trust is vital for successful manifestation, as it allows you to surrender control and believe that your desires will manifest in the best way possible.

6. **Fosters gratitude and contentment:** By detaching from specific outcomes, you can cultivate a sense of gratitude for the present moment and be content with what you have while still working toward your goals. This gratitude and contentment help raise your

vibration and attract more positive experiences into your life.

In summary, detachment is essential to the manifestation process because it helps reduce resistance, negative emotions, and attachment to specific outcomes. It allows you to trust in the Universe's ability to provide for your needs and opens a world of possibilities for manifesting your desires. Practicing detachment creates a more positive and receptive mindset, enhancing your ability to manifest your goals and achieve a more balanced and harmonious life.

BACK TO THE 12 LAWS

The Law of Attraction is well-known thanks to popular culture, but there are 11 other Laws that aren't given as much attention. These Laws are all focused on mastering your life with love and joy.

The first Law discussed in the next chapter is the Law of Divine Oneness. It emphasizes the interconnectedness of everything, including energy and the cosmos. Then, the Law of Vibration suggests that all matter, including ourselves, is perpetually moving and vibrating at a certain frequency that informs our daily experiences. The Law of Correspondence states that our reality is a reflection of what is happening within us because patterns repeat themselves throughout the Universe. The Law of Attraction, famously discussed in books like The Secret and The Alchemist, does not just highlight that like attracts like but also requires one to believe that what they aim for is possible.

The Law of Inspired Action encourages us to take the practical steps we need to move toward our manifested desires. Following that, the Law of Perpetual Transmutation of Energy asserts that our thoughts always precede our actions and that the energy in the Universe is continually changing. Similarly, the Law of Cause and Effect states that our actions directly correlate to events that happen afterward, while the Law of Compensation affirms that our positive efforts always come back to us in a similar way.

Our perspective shapes the meaning we derive from things since everything is essentially neutral, owing to the Law of Relativity. The Law of Polarity maintains that every aspect of life has an opposing force. Meanwhile, the Law of Rhythm makes us aware of the natural cycles that exist in the Universe and within ourselves, which means we can't expect to remain the same all the time. Lastly, the Law of Gender affirms that masculine and feminine energies are present in everything.

UP NEXT:

As we finish this first chapter, we should reflect on the concepts we have discussed so far. We delved into the enigma of the Universe, the energetic forces that bind everything together, and the significance of love in relation to it all. Through understanding our place in the cosmos, we've also explored ways to harness the positive energy around us for manifestation and making connections.

Take a moment to ponder what you've learned. What spoke to you the most? Did anything surprise you? Have you observed any of the 12 Laws at work in your own life now that you're aware of them? Reflection allows for a deeper understanding and integration of these concepts into one's life.

In the upcoming chapter, we'll dive deep into the Law of Divine Oneness—the idea that we are all interconnected and part of the same whole. This Law challenges the notion that we are separate beings and instead emphasizes our unity. As we explore this idea, we'll uncover how it can be harnessed for success and the manifestation of positive change. So, get ready to unlock the transformative power of interconnectedness.

2

THE LAW OF DIVINE ONENESS

All differences in this world are of degree, and not of kind, because oneness is the secret of everything.

— SWAMI VIVEKANANDA

THE DIVINE IN ME SEES THE DIVINE IN YOU

We are all interconnected as beings. Although we may perceive ourselves as separate entities, we are all composed of the same particles and elements originating from the same source of energy. Recognizing this interconnectedness can help us manifest our desires and reach our goals. By tapping into the energy of the Universe, which is beyond our individual selves, we can harness its power to work in our favor.

Divine Oneness and Manifestation

By focusing on our emotions and behavior, we can manifest the things that we desire and create a chain reaction of positive outcomes. The concept of interconnectedness can enable us to trigger positive effects in every aspect of our lives.

To instantly raise your vibration, think about what you are grateful for and feel that gratitude in your body; feel the love. It is essential to simplify the process and focus on what works. Identify areas where change is needed, embrace what is going well, and set positive intentions.

It is essential to understand that the Laws governing the Universe are not created by humans but are inherent in the workings of the Universe itself. These Laws are consistent and unchanging, and familiarizing yourself with them can help you manifest abundance in your life with greater ease.

A FOUNDATIONAL LAW

The fundamental Law of the Universe is the Law of Divine Oneness because it helps us understand the other Laws. It is the most elementary or basic Law, as it allows us to recognize the profound interconnectedness that exists between everything and everyone—including all the Laws of the Universe.

The Law of Divine Oneness is essential to understanding the other 11 Universal Laws, as they are all intertwined. These Laws are like different pieces of a puzzle that fit together to form a complete picture of the Universe. By thoroughly understanding the Law of Divine Oneness and applying it to our lives, we can begin to ascend to the next level of consciousness and unlock the limitless potential that lies within us.

Benefits of The Law of Divine Oneness

To reduce stress, aligning yourself with the surrounding environment and seeing yourself as one with all of creation is vital. This sense of unity will eliminate any feelings of separation between you and the world around you. Embrace the oneness that exists all around us and find ways to incorporate it into your everyday life to experience more peace, harmony, and spiritual growth while manifesting what you desire in a way that is filled with positivity.

HUMANITY AS A COLLECTIVE FAMILY

The Law of Divine Oneness reminds us that we are all connected as a family of humanity, spiritually supported and united equally. Connecting with someone we don't have a common bond or disagree with can sometimes be challenging. However, this is precisely where the Law of Divine Oneness comes into play, reminding us that we are all interconnected and that each interaction offers a chance for healing, awareness, reflection, and personal growth. We can return to a place of love, acceptance, and enjoyment of each other by raising our awareness and opening ourselves up to compassion, joy, support, gratitude, and appreciation.

Empathy

Empathy is the capacity to emotionally understand what others are feeling, seeing the world from their perspective, and experiencing their emotions as if they were our own. It involves recognizing and comprehending their emotions, adopting their viewpoint, using our own emotions as a reference, and genuinely sharing in their feelings. Empathy fosters deep connections, non-judgmental support, and effective communication, making it a vital element of building understanding and compassion among people. In the context of oneness, empathy underscores the interconnectedness of all beings by allowing us to connect on a profound emotional level, reminding us that our feelings and experiences are not isolated, but rather part of the shared human experience.

Signs

If you are someone who possesses empathetic tendencies, several signs may indicate this. For instance, you may find that people often share their problems with you, and you are good at really listening to what they have to say. You are also likely to pick up on other people's feelings and can be preoccupied with their emotional states. As a result, people approach you for advice because they sense that you are someone who cares about their well-being and will listen with an open mind.

At the same time, you may find tragic events and situations affecting you deeply and experience a sense of helplessness in such circumstances. However, you will typically try to help others who are suffering and do what you can to make things better. You may also be good at detecting when others are dishonest or not forthcoming with you. You can find it hard to set boundaries in your relationships because you care so deeply about other people's feelings.

Types:

There are three types of empathy that a person may experience, namely affective, somatic, and cognitive empathy.

- **Affective:** Affective empathy is the ability to comprehend the emotions of another and respond appropriately. It enables individuals to understand another person's feelings, which may lead to concern for their well-being or personal distress.
- **Somatic:** On the other hand, somatic empathy means physically reacting to someone else's situation. It's possible for individuals to have a physical experience of another person's emotions. For instance, when someone senses that another person is feeling embarrassed, they might start to blush or have an upset stomach.
- **Cognitive:** Cognitive empathy is the capacity to understand another person's mental state and what they might be thinking in response to the situation. It refers to the act of contemplating the thoughts of others.

Pitfalls

Empathy is a great trait to possess as it helps us to be concerned about the well-being and happiness of others. However, being highly empathetic can sometimes make us get overwhelmed or burnt out while always thinking about others' emotions. This exhaustion and emotional fatigue from repeated exposure to stressful or traumatic events is known as empathy fatigue. Research by Chikovani et al. (2015) has also shown that higher levels of empathy can lead to emotional negativity and increase the likelihood of empathic distress.

Impact

Empathy can have a significant impact on our relationships with others. Lam et al. (2012) found that siblings who have a high level of empathy for each other tend to have less conflict and more warmth in their interactions. Similarly, Kimmes and Durtschi (2016) found that having empathy in romantic relationships can increase our ability to forgive our partner. Genetics and socialization influence our ability to feel empathy, which shapes our beliefs and values toward others.

Barriers

Cognitive biases, dehumanization, and victim-blaming are among the factors that contribute to a lack of empathy. Some individuals may struggle with empathy, causing them to find it challenging to comprehend what others may be going through or feeling. Lack of empathy is also a prominent trait associated with narcissistic personality disorder (Baskin-Sommers et al., 2014).

- **Cognitive Biases:** Cognitive biases affect the way individuals view the world around them. One common bias is the tendency to attribute external failures to internal characteristics while blaming external factors for our own shortcomings.
- **Dehumanization:** It is easy to think that those different from us do not feel and behave in the same way we do. This is especially true when there is physical distance

between people. For instance, Cherry (2022) suggests that if someone watches a news report about a disaster or conflict in another country, they may be less likely to feel empathetic toward the individuals affected if they perceive them as fundamentally different from themselves.

- **Victim-Blaming:** People have the tendency to blame the victim for their misfortunes when they have experienced something traumatic or heartbreaking. This is evident when they ask the victims what they could have done differently to avoid the negative experience they encountered. The line of thinking comes from the innate desire to believe that the world is fair and just and that people get what they deserve and deserve what they get. However, this mindset can be misleading because it can make us believe that we are immune to such misfortunes and that terrible things could never happen to us.

Causes

Human beings are capable of acts of selfishness, cruelty, and insensitivity. Yet, not all individuals engage in these behaviors all the time. So what causes humans to feel empathy, the ability to feel another's pain, and respond with kindness? Over the years, various theories have been suggested to explain empathy:

- **Neuroscientific:** Recent studies have identified various brain areas that are critical to empathy, including the anterior cingulate cortex and the anterior insula.

Additionally, functional MRI research has shown that the inferior frontal gyrus (IFG) is also essential in the experience of empathy (Shamay-Tsoory et al., 2009). In fact, studies have revealed that individuals with damage to the IFG often struggle with recognizing emotions conveyed through facial expressions (Hillis, 2013).

- **Emotional:** One of the earliest reasons empathy was explored was to understand how people can have emotional experiences that they might not otherwise be able to feel. This can include feeling the emotions of others, whether real people or fictional characters.
- **Prosocial:** Empathy plays a role in the survival of the human species, according to sociologist Herbert Spencer (Cherry, 2022). This is because it leads to helping behavior, which in turn benefits social relationships. For example, someone witnessing a stranger in distress may empathize with that person's situation and be more likely to help.

Tips

If you would like to improve your empathy, there are many steps you can take. One is to maximize your ability to listen to others without interrupting them. Paying attention to body language and other nonverbal cues is also key. Additionally, try to actively understand the perspective of other people even when you disagree with them—asking questions about their experiences can be a valuable way to deepen your understanding of others. Imagine yourself in another person's shoes and try to see things from their point of view. It's also essential to do the work to recognize any biases you may have and how they might affect your empathy toward others. Rather than focusing on differences between yourself and others, try to find common ground. Have the courage to open and express your own emotion. Finally, getting involved with organizations that promote social change can offer valuable opportunities to broaden your perspectives.

USING THE LAW OF DIVINE ONENESS FOR A BETTER LIFE

Meet Alex

Alex, a once-busy corporate executive, embarked on a transformative journey by embracing the Law of Oneness. Through daily mindfulness meditation, Alex became more attuned to their connection with the world. They nurtured relationships with family and friends, fostering a deeper sense of belonging. Recognizing their connection to the environment, Alex adopted a sustainable lifestyle and engaged in community service, amplifying their sense of unity with fellow citizens. A career shift toward purpose-driven work and the cultivation of empathy and compassion further deepened Alex's newfound sense of interconnectedness. As a result, their life became more balanced, meaningful, and harmonious, demonstrating the profound positive impact of embracing the Law of Oneness.

Tips

The Law of Divine Oneness is a universal Law that transcends race, religion, and culture. It's a powerful tool that you can use to improve the quality of your life. Here are some ways you can use it:

- Time is an invaluable resource. Embrace the present moment, take purposeful action, and use your time wisely to maximize its potential. Avoid waiting for circumstances to change, and remember to let go of the things you can't control.
- When dealing with negative people, don't let their energy bring you down. Instead, redirect your focus to something positive. Respond with kindness and positivity, even when it's not easy.
- See others as a reflection of the divine oneness they are a part of. Focus on their unique gifts and abilities rather than judging them for their past actions. Treat others as you would like to be treated.
- Recognize that you are one with your environment. Everything is connected, so make sure you treat the world around you with respect and care.
- Remember that we are all equal—regardless of status, wealth, or experience. Let go of any judgments or prejudices you may have toward others.
- To truly benefit from the Law of Divine Oneness, you must be in a state of grace. This Law is a spiritual philosophy and practice that requires a connection with a higher power.
- Finally, remember that the Law of Divine Oneness is not a quick fix or a magical solution to all your problems. However, it can bring about profound changes within you and help you to reach your full

potential. Take responsibility for your actions and strive to be the best version of yourself.

Application in Everyday Life

The Law of Divine Oneness is not just a theoretical concept but something that can be applied in practical ways to everyday life. First, we need to learn to accept ourselves and those around us as part of creation and connected to the whole Universe. Secondly, we should prioritize our time, focusing on what is most important, like helping others and pursuing personal growth. When dealing with differences, we must not take them personally but seek commonalities instead. Forgiveness is also crucial when others don't meet our expectations or disagree with us. Treating everyone equally regardless of their background is important, and we must avoid discrimination as it only hurts us in the end. Finally, we should disregard negative opinions and share positive energy with those around us.

ACTION STEPS

- Nurture a feeling of unity by establishing connections with others and assisting them in their pursuit of realizing their aspirations.
- Take some time to meditate on the connection that exists between you and a person whom you may not feel particularly drawn toward spiritually. Your goal is cultivating empathy, so endeavor to view this individual from a commonality perspective, in which you share a universal bond.

- To cultivate gratitude, take time to contemplate the abundance and positive aspects of your life. Show your appreciation by performing acts of kindness toward others.
- To improve your manifestation skills, develop your self-awareness. Pay attention to your thoughts and emotions in order to recognize any beliefs or thought patterns that may be restricting you. By identifying these limitations, you can begin to work on shifting your mindset and manifesting your true desires.
- To cultivate a sense of oneness with the Universe, it's important not to feel overwhelmed or burdened with the task of fully comprehending it. Rather, understand that you are already a part of it and connected to everything.

UP NEXT:

In this chapter, we delved into the concept of the Law of Divine Oneness and explored how it can be used to achieve success. This Universal Law is fundamental, and we discussed its benefits in detail. It also emphasizes the importance of connecting with others, even those who seem different from us, in order to foster a sense of oneness among humanity.

The Law of Divine Oneness highlights the importance of empathy, which allows us to connect with others at a deeper level. It can help us understand and relate to others in a meaningful way. However, it's essential to be aware that empathy can also have negative consequences. Therefore, we must find a balance between being empathic and caring for ourselves.

To manifest our dreams and goals, we must set positive intentions grounded in empathy and align ourselves with the energy of the Universe—this is where the next Law, the Law of Vibration, comes in. This Law teaches us that everything is made up of energy, and we have the power to attract things we desire by matching their energy. The next chapter will explore the Law of Vibration in more detail and provide practical tips for harnessing its power to manifest our desires.

3

THE LAW OF VIBRATION

If you want to find the secrets of the Universe, think in terms of energy, frequency, and vibration.

— NIKOLA TESLA

VIBRATING HIGHER

I was brought up in the Catholic faith and had a strong connection with God. I always believed that things would work out. However, my faith wavered when faced with challenging circumstances, and I spiraled into addiction. The more I dwelled on my problems, the more they intensified. It was only after finding recovery that I rediscovered my faith. I began to explore the laws of the Universe and incorporate them into my daily life.

I started to pay attention to the signs that came my way and took healthy risks whenever opportunities presented themselves. Additionally, I shifted my focus toward gratitude and giving, which allowed abundance to flow into my life. Although I still experience setbacks, I concentrate on finding solutions and letting go of things beyond my control.

For instance, when my mother passed away unexpectedly, I discovered solace in believing she would always be with me. She sends me signs every day as a reminder to reinforce this belief. This experience motivated me to write my first book, The Spiritual Meanings of Numbers.

My unyielding faith and adoration for the Universe are a source of gratitude for me. Through my struggles, I have come to firmly believe that my life has a unique purpose in this vast Universe. As a result, I have been able to experience continuous growth and positive changes in my life by maintaining trust in the Universe and being receptive to its guidance.

As I continued to practice, I noticed a shift in my reality. I attracted new opportunities and connections that aligned with my goals and desires. My career took off, and I found a sense of purpose I had been missing for so long. It was amazing to see how the Universe seemed to be working in my favor.

I came to understand that the Law of Vibration wasn't just a vague theory but a powerful force that could transform my life. By aligning my energy with my desires, I could attract them into my life. So today, I live with deep gratitude and unwavering faith in the laws of the Universe.

GOOD VIBRATIONS

While the Law of Vibration has been a widely accepted concept for centuries, it has recently gained popularity due to rising interest in the Law of Attraction. The Law of Vibration states that everything in the Universe is made up of energy and has a unique frequency or vibration. Every object, thought, and emotion has its own specific vibration. Different outcomes are produced in the physical world as these energies interact and collide.

Understanding the concept of vibration and how to align yourself with it is essential for successful manifestation. Vibration refers to the energy frequency that surrounds us, and plays a significant role in attracting our desires. To manifest your dreams, you must make sure that your thoughts, emotions, and actions are all in harmony with the vibration of what you desire.

The Law of Vibration

Vibrational frequency is a crucial concept in understanding the science of energy and vibration. It refers to the speed at which the atoms in our cells move, ultimately affecting our physical, emotional, and mental well-being. At a fundamental level, our entire being, including all living beings and inanimate objects, consists of cells made up of atoms. The frequency of anything determines the speed at which its vibrational pattern occurs. If something vibrates quickly, it possesses a higher vibration; if it moves at a slower pace, it has a lower vibration.

What Is It?

The Law of Vibration is a principle that suggests that our thoughts, feelings, habits, and desires all vibrate at a particular frequency. Whether it's visible or not, this means that everything in our Universe has an energetic configuration. We need to resonate at the same vibrational frequency as our desires to manifest something into our life. We can create a harmonious vibration that draws the desired outcome toward us by aligning our thoughts and emotions with what we want. This Law applies to everything in our lives, from relationships to career goals and personal aspirations. By aligning our vibrations with our desires, we can attract anything we want into our lives.

Vibration and Intuition

Your body has a powerful ability to tune in to the emotional states of others. This keen sensitivity was vital for our survival in the past, allowing us to assess potential danger quickly. However, many of us have become disconnected from this innate gift. We can tap into the Law of Vibration and make more intuitive decisions by paying attention to the subtle feelings and sensations within us. These signals may take the form of a prickling sensation or an uneasiness in the stomach when faced with a particular situation (Brown, 2021b). Even though we all have free will, we can create a more rewarding and purposeful existence by choosing to follow our intuition and attune ourselves to the energy around us.

How Vibration Affects You

Vibration can significantly impact various aspects of our lives. So let's explore some of them together:

Vibration and Abundance

When you actively work on raising your vibrational frequency, you become more open to receiving abundance in your life. This is because a higher frequency puts you in a state of present-moment awareness and heightened consciousness, allowing you to notice opportunities and resources that may have previously gone unnoticed.

Similar energies tend to attract each other. So, as you continue to maintain a high vibrational frequency and live in a state of positive energy, you will naturally begin to attract more abundance, positivity, and fulfillment into your life. This is a process that requires consistent effort and focus, but the rewards are well worth it. By raising your vibration, you can begin to experience a life filled with abundance, joy, and limitless possibility.

Vibration and Happiness

Our mood is greatly affected by our vibrational frequency. The higher our vibration, the better our mood becomes. And the happier we are, the higher our vibe is raised. Essentially, our happiness and vibration levels are directly proportional to each other.

To increase our vibration, we must focus on positive thoughts and feelings. When we think and, more importantly, feel positivity, our vibe automatically goes up, leading to a more joyful and content state of mind. Moreover, our high vibe is contagious and spreads to the people around us. As we radiate positive energy and good vibes, we influence those around us, making them feel better as well.

Vibration and Creation

If you aim to tailor your life according to your desires, you need to keep a close look at your energy. One must maintain a high level of positive energy to manifest their dream life effectively. Even though people believe that the Law of Attraction is the ultimate tool for manifesting their dreams, it is not always the case. You must focus on your vibration to achieve your desired outcome through attraction. Therefore, the key to manifestation is vibration. You need to think and speak good vibes to yourself and those around you to raise your vibration.

Vibration and Consciousness

Being aware of the present moment is crucial as it connects you to the energy and vibrations of your surroundings. Many people go through life without paying attention to certain details, and that's why they attract unnecessary drama into their lives. Remaining present in every moment helps you see beyond the surface of people's actions and behaviors and recognize the energy behind them.

When you are conscious of the current moment, you can easily feel the energy that surrounds you. Your consciousness and vibrational frequency work in unison. To feel the vibration of people and things around you, it's important to stay focused on the present. This heightened awareness can help you decide who to interact with and who to avoid, making your interactions healthy and meaningful.

Use the Law of Vibration to Your Advantage

Manifesting

Manifestation is based on the principle of matching vibrations. In basic terms, this means that in order to attract something into your life, you need to align your energy with the energy of that thing. This is because everything in the Universe vibrates at a specific frequency, and we have the power to control our own energy frequency through our thoughts.

For example, if you want to manifest more money but constantly worry about how much you need it, you are emitting a vibration of lack and scarcity. This can actually block the Universe from bringing you the abundance you desire. Therefore, focusing on thoughts and feelings that align with prosperity and abundance is essential, such as gratitude for the money you already have. Imagine yourself living the life you want and believe it is already yours.

Navigating

The Universal Law of Vibration can be a helpful tool in determining how you feel in various situations or scenarios. By tuning in to what feels high-vibrational to you, such as positive attitudes, uplifting environments, and inspiring people, you can better sense when you are in the presence of high vibes. This awareness allows you to make conscious choices about where you invest your energy and attention, ultimately leading to a more fulfilling and joyful life.

Emotions

Emotions are also subject to this Law since they also possess vibrational frequencies. Negative emotions such as fear and shame reside at a lower frequency. In contrast, positive emotions like love and joy exist at higher frequencies. While it may seem like some emotions are "bad," all emotions are simply energy that needs to be released.

By becoming aware of the Law of vibration, we can learn to recognize when we're feeling heavy, negative emotions and allow them to pass through us. The Law of Vibration can help us shift from a lower state of being to a higher, more balanced state of mind. Emotions bring feelings that are powerful guides, which can help us live a more fulfilling and joyful life.

RAISE YOUR VIBRATION

Regularly practicing self-care can raise your vibration and help you show up more clearly and strongly in the world. Self-care can look different for everyone, whether it be through taking a weekly bath ritual, prioritizing time in nature, or journaling (Regan, 2021). By following a high-vibrational diet and engaging in regular physical activity, you can experience a lightness of energy and avoid feeling weighed down.

Find daily activities that make you feel good and balanced, focusing on joy, love, and peace. Of course, what these activities are will also vary for everyone, but focusing on these vibrations can help us feel happier and healthier.

Nourishing your body with a high-vibrational diet and movement routine can leave you feeling energetically light and not bogged down. Unhealthy foods can lower our energy, and a lack of exercise can make us feel stagnant. However, a good workout can leave us feeling energized.

Engaging in meditation can enhance our capacity to regulate emotions, release attachments, and elevate our energetic frequency. With so many different types of meditation available, it's important to discover what works for you.

The impact of the external world on your energetic frequency should not be underestimated. Avoid people, places, and things that drain your energy whenever possible. While it's not always possible to completely cut low-vibrational situations out of our lives, avoiding them when we can help protect the high frequency we've been cultivating. As you work with the Law of Vibration, you'll be better equipped to steady your vibe, regardless of outside influence.

Meet Sarah

Grappling with chronic stress and negativity, Sarah discovered the Law of Vibration and decided to apply it to her life. She shifted her mindset, embraced a healthier lifestyle, and spent more time with uplifting people and positive groups. Through visualization, daily affirmations, and gratitude practice, she raised her vibrational frequency. Over time, this led to reduced stress, improved relationships, and attracting opportunities aligned with her positive energy. Sarah's journey exemplified how aligning thoughts and emotions with higher vibrational frequencies, combined with positive connections, can lead to a more fulfilling life.

ACTION STEPS

- Take note of your thoughts and emotions to practice mindfulness. Concentrate on the ones that boost your energy level and match this with your intended goals.
- Reflect on what low-vibrational situations or people may be draining your energy.
- Draw in favorable experiences and people by utilizing positive affirmations. Enhance your positive energy by shifting your mindset. If it makes you feel good, do more of that.
- Look for activities or experiences that boost your energy, like being in natural surroundings, listening to inspirational music, or spending quality time with loved ones who bring positivity to your life.
- Raise your vibration and attract positive energy into your life by practicing self-care on a regular basis.

UP NEXT:

In this chapter, we have expanded on the concepts of physics related to matters that we previously discussed in relation to the Law of Divine Oneness. The Law of Vibration is a scientifically established principle that suggests that everything in the Universe is composed of energy and has a unique frequency or vibration. This principle is closely related to the Law of Attraction, which proposes that we can manifest our desires by aligning our energy with our goals.

We have explored various ways in which the Law of Vibration can impact us and how to utilize it to our advantage. By elevating our vibration and avoiding low-vibration situations whenever feasible, we can increase our energy levels and align them with our desired outcomes. This entails ensuring that our thoughts, feelings, and actions are in harmony and that we emit a high-frequency vibration corresponding with what we wish to attract into our lives.

Next, we continue to build upon the first two Laws by examining the Law of Correspondence, which states that there is an interconnectedness and harmony between different levels of existence. This includes the physical, mental, and spiritual dimensions. Essentially, what we observe in the external world reflects within ourselves, our thoughts, and our experiences. By applying and understanding this Law, individuals can gain deeper awareness and understanding of their inner and outer worlds. It can help uncover personal meaning and purpose and encourage balance and harmony in one's life. In essence, the Law of Correspondence offers a deeply profound opportunity to cultivate a holistic approach to living your life and manifesting your dreams.

4

THE LAW OF CORRESPONDENCE

As above, so below. As within, so without.

— HERMES TRISMEGISTUS

CARBON COPY

The Law of Correspondence is a principle that states that there is correspondence between the physical and spiritual realms. This Law suggests that everything in the Universe is connected and a relationship exists between the seen and unseen worlds.

The quote "As above, so below. As within, so without" is a fundamental concept in the Law of Correspondence. It suggests that there is a relationship between the inner and outer worlds, as well as between the larger Universe and the individual. In other words, what happens on one level is reflected on another, and vice versa.

The correspondence paradox is a common concern when we consider the idea that we create our own experiences (Oberlin, 2017). It raises questions such as, should we be held responsible for other people's unkind behavior, violent conflicts, natural disasters, or illnesses? However, if we believe that external circumstances solely determine our emotions, we may feel like a victim of our circumstances. Although it is understandable, this mindset is disempowering in the long run.

There are two ways to use our consciousness to address this challenge. The first is to view life from an energetic perspective, where certain emotions resonate at different frequencies—as discussed in the previous chapter. The second is to consider life from a spiritual perspective, using challenging events as opportunities for self-reflection and growth. This involves asking ourselves big questions about our personal experiences, traumas, beliefs, and their impact on our well-being. By doing so, we can address imbalances within ourselves and improve our relationships with others.

WORLD OF MIRRORS

The Law of Correspondence posits that the state of our external reality is a reflection of our internal state, meaning that our thoughts, beliefs, and emotions shape the world around us. Every thought, feeling, and intention we hold within ourselves has a corresponding effect on the external world.

Therefore, if our lives are filled with dissatisfaction, confusion, or despair, it is because we are emitting negative energy from within. This negative energy can manifest in many ways, such as negative self-talk, limiting beliefs, or unresolved emotional wounds. On the other hand, if we cultivate positive thoughts, beliefs, and emotions, our external reality will reflect these states.

How It Works

The Law of Correspondence has the potential to transform your life in many ways. Understanding this Law allows you to master various manifestation techniques and create your desired reality. Because this Law suggests that physical reality is a projection of our minds, the external world will reflect what we think and feel inside. The outer world does not mirror only our best self; it reflects all our mind's contents, including any negative thoughts, beliefs, and assumptions. However, the Law of Correspondence is not meant to be discouraging. Rather, it is a call to action—it is a reminder that we have the power to create the reality we desire by consciously choosing our thoughts, beliefs, and emotions.

Paradigm Shift

The concept of "as above, so below" highlights the correlation between our internal state and external reality. If we feel negative or toxic on the inside, this negativity will also manifest in our external reality. This cycle can be challenging to break, but it is possible by utilizing the Law of Correspondence.

To shift this toxic cycle, we must begin by changing our internal state to align with the principles of this Law. By making a total paradigm shift, we can transform our entire reality simply by changing our perspective. The Law of Correspondence works because external change can only occur if it begins internally.

To initiate this transformation, we must first identify the negative thoughts, beliefs, and emotions fueling the toxic cycle. Then, by addressing these internal issues and replacing them with positive, life-affirming beliefs, we can shift our state and attract more positivity into our external reality.

Four Things to Change

To harness the power of the Law of Correspondence and create a transformation in your physical world, there are four essential components that you must address: your attitude, beliefs, thoughts, and feelings.

Firstly, your attitude toward life and yourself plays a crucial role in shaping your reality. Therefore, shifting your attitude toward a more positive and optimistic outlook is essential to attract positive change into your life.

Secondly, your beliefs are a fundamental aspect of your inner world that influences your external reality. If you hold limiting beliefs that prevent you from achieving your goals or living your best life, you will attract situations that validate those beliefs.

Finally, your thoughts are a powerful force that shapes your reality. Your thoughts create your emotions, which cause your feelings.

On Thoughts

Our perception of events and the way we interpret them is influenced by our beliefs and self-concept, which in turn shapes our reality. This process creates a story in our minds that can become a self-fulfilling prophecy, reinforcing our beliefs through our actions. Our brains have a selective filtering system that reinforces our beliefs by focusing mostly on information consistent with them (Vilhauer, 2020). Accepting that our perception and interpretation create our reality empowers us to be in charge of our lives, even though there are many aspects of life we cannot control.

Taking Control

Our thoughts have the power to transform our lives. We hold complete control over this element as the authors of our own life. Our thoughts represent a higher energy level, while our physical body represents a lower energy level. Applying the Law of Correspondence here means that our thoughts can manifest into our physical reality.

Unfortunately, when we face hardship, we often blame external factors. This is a defense mechanism that avoids admitting that we are the problem. To transform our lives, we must accept our shortcomings and work to change them; to take charge of our lives, we must take control of our minds.

The Butterfly Effect

According to the Law of Correspondence, our existence is composed of three dimensions—physical, mental, and spiritual. To achieve our fullest potential, we must ensure that these planes are in harmony. They are interconnected and in constant communication.

A butterfly's wings create energy waves that reverberate throughout the Universe—this is called the Butterfly Effect. Our beliefs, thoughts, and feelings create similar waves that influence our existence. At the macro level, our reality is constructed from our micro-level experiences. Therefore, every action we take has a ripple effect that impacts our overall behavior. Even the smallest act can significantly impact the structure of our behavior. Ultimately, we are all connected, and our actions have consequences that reverberate throughout the Universe.

CREATING FROM AN INTERNAL ENVIRONMENT

Do you find yourself stuck in a cycle encountering similar problems over and over again? This might be a sign to change your internal environment. In order to make the Law of Correspondence work for us, we need to be intentional about where we place our energy. If something isn't working in our lives, we need to look within and assess where we might be giving too much energy to negative thoughts and emotions. This means taking responsibility for our own emotions and mindset and being willing to make changes to align ourselves with our desired reality.

Correspondence by Association

The Law of Correspondence emphasizes the importance of being aware of what you allow around you, as it affects what shows up within you. This involves paying attention to the things you consume and deciding if they align with the identity you want to create. You become the energetic average of what you surround yourself with. There's no need for perfection, but you should take inventory of whether your correspondence scales lean toward positivity or negativity. You can counteract things that drain you by doing something that brings you back into alignment.

Emotions and the Law of Correspondence

The Law of Correspondence highlights the role of our internal environment in constantly creating our reality. Our emotional nature plays a crucial part in shaping how we view things and assign meaning. For example, when feeling good, we tend to accept compliments gracefully and believe them genuinely, reinforcing our positive emotional state. Conversely, when in a bad mood, the same compliment may be perceived as insincere or sarcastic, projecting our internal narratives onto our surroundings. However, as soon as we become aware of this projection, we can choose to change it without waiting.

Manifesting With the Law of Correspondence

One of the most effective ways to manifest what you desire is by shifting your internal environment, and one way to do this is by practicing appreciation. The energy you put into the practice of appreciation is the energy you receive from it. Look for moments throughout the day when feeling appreciative and lean into that feeling to stay there longer. For example, if a friend does something thoughtful, take the time to really feel your appreciation and love for them. How do you feel afterward?

Over time, this practice will train your brain to feel gratitude naturally, and it will become a natural state of being. In addition, you will start to notice that these situations will occur more frequently, providing you with more opportunities to express gratitude.

How the Law of Correspondence Can Work Against Us

There's no one right way to manifest your desires—follow what resonates with you. However, using your knowledge of the Law of Correspondence is important to avoid attracting what you don't want. Focusing on fear and scarcity only invites more negativity into our lives. Instead, remember that our inner world creates our outer reality.

To truly harness the power of manifestation, it's crucial to look inward and focus on healing ourselves. This means paying attention to our emotional responses, bodily sensations, perceptions, and reactions. Self-reflection and emotional resiliency are key ingredients to creating the life you desire. It's also important to identify and break free from limiting beliefs.

Remember, changing your outer world starts with changing your inner world. Be aware of your thoughts, emotions, and behaviors, and break negative cycles. As you cultivate positive thoughts and emotions, your reality will reflect your inner state, and you'll start to see your dreams manifest into reality.

Meet John

John confronted challenges in his long-term relationship, realizing it had become strained over time. Embracing the Law of Correspondence, he understood that the quality of external relationships often mirrors inner dynamics. Through self-reflection and personal growth, John addressed unresolved issues and negative thought patterns stemming from past traumas that had been affecting both his life and his relationship. He took accountability for his behavior, recognizing that his unresolved personal issues were influencing his actions within the relationship. Committed to better communication, he practiced active listening and engaged in open dialogue. John also embarked on a courageous journey to face, heal, and let go of his past in order to create a better future. Over time, his relationship transformed, reflecting the power of aligning inner growth with external circumstances, resulting in improved communication and a stronger, more fulfilling partnership.

APPLYING THE LAW OF CORRESPONDENCE: TIPS FOR CREATING THE LIFE YOU WANT

- **Observe your thoughts and feelings:** Our predominant thoughts and feelings determine the effects occurring in our lives. Therefore, noticing and observing our thought patterns is essential, as they can be limiting and stem from past experiences. In addition, by examining our thoughts and perceptions in all aspects of life, we can identify and replace negative beliefs and behaviors.

- **Accept responsibility:** To shape your reality, take responsibility for your thoughts and beliefs. When a negative thought enters your mind, counteract it by intentionally focusing on three positive thoughts instead. Transform limiting questions into expensive ones. Instead of asking, "Why can't I do this?" which can create a sense of defeat, we can ask, "How can I accomplish this?"

- **Keep a journal:** Journaling is a powerful tool for reflecting on experiences and tracking progress. Writing down thoughts and feelings helps gain insight into the inner world and identify thinking patterns. Use a journal to declare positive thoughts, write goals and aspirations, and express gratitude. Regularly recording things to be thankful for cultivates a positive mindset and appreciation for abundance.

- **Practice gratitude:** Cultivating an attitude of gratitude can have a powerful impact on your emotional and mental well-being. When you focus on the things in your life that you are grateful for, you are shifting your attention away from what is lacking or negative toward what you already have. In addition, feeling a sense of gratitude can create opportunities for even more things to feel grateful for.

- **Look for opportunities to feel positive:** Seek positive experiences to develop a more optimistic outlook.

Instead of dwelling on mistakes or shortcomings, identify constructive lessons you can learn. Focus on the positive aspects and view the situation as a valuable learning experience.

- **Visualization:** You have the power to create the future you desire. Visualizing your goals and dreams can ignite a fire within you, driving you toward success with a newfound passion. Don't allow your present reality to limit what you believe is possible for yourself. With the power of visualization, you can shatter those limitations and create a clear path to your dreams. But remember, visualization is just the starting point. It's crucial to take action toward your goals by breaking them down into achievable tasks. Every step forward is a step toward a better tomorrow. So believe in yourself, take action, feel good, and make your dreams a reality.

ACTION STEPS

- To align your thoughts and beliefs with your desired outcomes, try creating a vision board or a visualization exercise.
- Think of an example of a limiting belief you hold about yourself and reframe it to focus on positive possibilities.
- Practicing a loving-kindness meditation can help you release negative energy and blockages that may be hindering your ability to manifest your desires while sending positive energy and compassion to yourself and others.

- Consider the attitude you have toward yourself. How could you change it to be more positive? It may help to view yourself from the point of view of a friend.
- Practicing self-reflection can be beneficial in identifying any negative thoughts or beliefs that could potentially hinder your progress. Replace these with positive and empowering ones to move toward manifesting your desires.

UP NEXT:

The Law of Correspondence teaches that our internal world creates our external reality. Our thoughts, emotions, and beliefs determine the circumstances we attract into our lives. By accepting and embracing this principle, we can take control of our inner dialogue and adjust it to align with our desired outcomes.

Positive thinking is one of the best practices to align our thoughts and emotions with our goals. With practice and perseverance, we can retrain our minds to think positively and manifest the outcomes we desire. Gratitude is another essential practice for applying the Law of Correspondence. By expressing gratitude for what we have and encounter, and more importantly, genuinely feeling grateful for it, we cultivate a sense of abundance and attract more positive experiences.

Taking responsibility for our thoughts and emotions is also crucial for effectively applying the Law of Correspondence. This means acknowledging that we have the power to choose our thoughts and emotions and are responsible for the outcomes we attract into our lives.

The Law of Correspondence builds upon the Law of Vibration, which teaches us that everything in the Universe is energy and that our thoughts and emotions emit vibrations that attract similar energies. Therefore, by attuning ourselves to higher frequencies of positivity, we can manifest our desires and connect with our higher selves in harmony with the Universe.

Moving forward, we will explore the Law of Attraction, which is the most popular and fundamental Law of the Universe. This Law is based on the principle that our thoughts and emotions have a powerful influence on the circumstances we attract into our lives. Therefore, by maintaining a focus on positive thoughts and emotions, we can manifest our goals and aspirations and live the life we desire.

5

THE LAW OF ATTRACTION

What you seek is seeking you.

— RUMI

CASE STUDY

J enny used to have a negative perspective on life. She felt surrounded by problems and overwhelmed by challenges, making it extremely difficult to recognize any positivity in her life. Noticing her struggles, a friend introduced her to the Law of Attraction and said it could help her shift her negative mindset into a positive one.

Intrigued by the concept, she decided to give it a try. She began by listing down all the things she was grateful for, no matter how small they seemed. Instead of focusing on negative aspects, she tried to focus on positive ones. Then, to further practice the Law of Attraction, she started visualizing her ideal life. She created a vision board with pictures and affirmations that helped represent her goals and desires. Every day, she would focus on this vision, truly believing it was possible for her to achieve and feeling that belief deep within herself.

As Jenny kept practicing the Law of Attraction daily, she noticed a shift in her mindset. She started feeling more hopeful and optimistic about her future and began attracting more positive experiences into her life. Her relationships improved, and she found herself in situations that brought her joy and fulfillment.

Jenny received a job offer for her ideal position, which she had been visualizing and affirming for weeks. She almost couldn't believe it, but she knew that the power of the Law of Attraction brought this opportunity into her life. Since then, she has realized that by focusing on positivity and gratitude, she could create a life full of joy, abundance, and fulfillment. As a result, she continues to practice the Law of Attraction, inspiring others to do the same as her friend did for her.

THE LAW EXPLAINED

Jenny's story exemplifies the power of the Law of Attraction. By focusing on positive thoughts and emotions, she was able to transform her life and attract opportunities that aligned with her goals. This concept is based on the belief that our thoughts and emotions shape our reality, and by staying positive and taking action toward our goals, we can achieve success. Of course, it's essential to maintain a balanced perspective and acknowledge that setbacks and challenges will arise. However, we can learn and grow from these experiences by embracing personal growth and cultivating positivity. In other words, what we think about and feel on a consistent basis is what we ultimately manifest in our lives.

What Is It?

The Law of Attraction gained widespread attention through Rhonda Byrne's book The Secret, which popularized the Law and its potential to transform lives (Eatough, 2023). At the heart of this philosophy is the power of positivity. Research has indicated that a positive attitude can significantly affect our physical and mental health. Positive thinking has been linked to better physical health, longer life, and a reduced risk of heart disease. Additionally, cultivating a growth mindset can have mental health benefits, such as reducing anxiety and depression and helping to manage stress.

There are several methods that can assist us in adopting a more positive perspective. Positive self-talk involves using affirmations and positive statements to build our self-esteem and promote a more positive mindset. Visualization involves imagining ourselves in positive scenarios and experiencing the emotions associated with those situations. Finally, cognitive bias adjustments involve challenging negative thoughts and reframing them in a more positive light.

By embracing change and maintaining a positive emotional state, we can develop new skills and ultimately achieve greater success. Additionally, we may experience increased mindfulness, gratitude, and self-compassion. Acknowledging our reality and accepting that the world doesn't always work in our favor is crucial. We will face setbacks and challenges, but maintaining a positive outlook can help us overcome these obstacles more easily. Look for the lesson and solution instead of dwelling on the problem. This proactive approach allows us to learn and grow from our experiences, creating a stronger foundation for future success.

How Does It Work?

The Law of Attraction can be understood in different ways, but the core principles remain the same. It's all about staying positive, feeling that positivity, and taking action toward our goals, no matter what they may be. We need more than focus on what we want; we must also do something about it. To do this, we must prioritize our mental health, set realistic goals, establish a routine, and embrace personal growth.

Seven Laws

The Law of Attraction implies that the energy we emit into the world attracts similar energy back to us. Under this Law, there are seven lesser laws that contain lessons to help individuals improve their lives by cultivating positivity and drawing in more positive experiences.

The first Law is Magnetism, which suggests that our thoughts and emotions have a powerful impact on the experiences we attract. By focusing on positive thoughts and emotions, we attract more positive experiences; by concentrating on the negative ones, more negative experiences come our way.

The second Law is Manifestation, which encourages us to focus on the present and take action toward the future we desire. Instead of dwelling on the past or worrying about the future, we need to act in the present moment to reach our goals.

The third Law is about Right Action, which vitalizes the need to eliminate negative aspects in our lives leading to unfulfillment. We should remove these negative elements and replace them with positive experiences and opportunities.

The fourth Law is Delicate Balance, which acknowledges that life's setbacks and failures are normal. Rather than being disheartened, we should learn from them and celebrate our wins.

The fifth Law, Unwavering Desires, emphasizes staying focused on our goals and desires. Even though our lives change and evolve, we should remain resilient to our values and desires to achieve our most important goals.

The sixth Law is Harmony, which recognizes that the people and energy around us can impact our outlook and success. By surrounding ourselves with positive, supportive people, we can maintain a positive mindset and achieve greater success.

Finally, the seventh Law, Universal Influence, emphasizes the importance of our actions and how they impact the experiences we attract. By treating others with respect and kindness, we invite positive energy and experiences into our lives.

The Law of Attraction's Perfect Partner

The Law of Assumption, often regarded as a complementary principle to the Law of Attraction, emphasizes the influential role of our beliefs and assumptions in shaping our reality. While the Law of Attraction is centered around the idea that our thoughts and emotions magnetize experiences that resonate with their vibrational energy, the Law of Assumption goes a step further by focusing on the transformative power of belief and conviction.

The Law of Assumption posits that when we wholeheartedly embrace the feeling of our desires and confidently assume their manifestation, we actively participate in the creation of our own lives, turning aspirations into tangible experiences.

When working in tandem, the Law of Attraction and the Law of Assumption create a potent synergy for personal growth and success. The Law of Attraction magnetizes opportunities and circumstances in line with our thoughts and emotions. The Law of Assumption ensures that our beliefs and convictions pave the way for the desired outcome.

Together, these laws enable us to harness our inner power, seize control of our destiny, and unlock our limitless potential. By consciously aligning our thoughts, emotions, and beliefs, we can effectively shape our lives according to our desires and aspirations, guided by the harmonious interplay of these universal principles.

THE SCIENCE BEHIND THE LAW OF ATTRACTION

Quantum physics offers a probable explanation for the feasibility of the Law of Attraction. Max Planck, one of the founding fathers of quantum physics, once said (Singh, 2020):

"There is no matter as such! All matter originates and exists only by virtue of a force which brings the particles of an atom to vibration and holds this most minute solar system of the atom together... We must assume behind this force the existence of a conscious and intelligent Mind. This Mind is the matrix of all matter."

This intelligent mind is the entity our ancestors referred to as infinite consciousness. The science behind the Law of Attraction is explained by the idea that we can influence the Universe through our thoughts and intentions. It works by using five simple steps:

- Getting clarity on your outcome
- Getting in a gratitude state
- Visualizing the outcome
- Genuinely feeling that belief at a deep level within yourself
- Surrendering the outcome to greater intelligence

Scientific Proof of the Law of Attraction

Platonic Roots

The Law of Attraction's fundamental message, that "like attracts like," closely resembles a statement made by the renowned

Greek philosopher Plato in 391 BC: "likes tend towards likes" (Hurst, 2016).

Medical Journals

In 2007, the Yonsei Medical Journal provided a notable instance of scientific evidence supporting the Law of Attraction (Jung et al., 2007). Korean researchers, including Ji Young Jung, discovered a significant correlation between positive thinking and general life satisfaction among the population. These results align with the views of academics who recommend positive thinking exercises to enhance the likelihood of manifestation.

Neurology

Scientists at London's Institute of Neurology found that visualizing a better future can increase the likelihood of achieving it (Hurst, 2016). This supports the Law of Attraction, which suggests that clear and frequent mental imagery of a better life can draw it toward us.

Psychology

A University of Exeter researcher found that repeatedly affirming one's ability to achieve a goal increases the likelihood of a positive outcome (Hurst, 2016). Affirmations are also beneficial for recovery from trauma, anticipatory planning, depression treatment, and physical health.

Mirror Neurons

Cultivating a positive mindset and emitting high-frequency vibrations is essential to practice the Law of Attraction. The phenomenon is partly due to mirror neurons that mimic observed behavior, leading to positive reactions toward you.

Genetics

New genetic research shows that negative beliefs that hinder manifestation are not entirely your fault. Scientists in Atlanta found that mice can pass their fear to their offspring through genetic code, even if they didn't experience the trauma themselves (Eastman, 2013).

SYNCHRONICITIES

Synchronicity is the occurrence of seemingly unrelated events that share a meaningful connection. Science shows that synchronicities happen when vibrational energies are in alignment (Whitman, 2022). The Universe is made of energy, and the Law of Attraction draws like energies together. In my book, *From The Universe With Love*, I emphasized the significance of receptivity to signs, writing, "Receptivity is very important. Keep your mind open, your senses calm, and your vibrations high. You will receive, never doubt that!" (Motley, 2021b). This understanding allows us to recognize synchronicities as natural byproducts of the Universe's energetic movement.

How Does Synchronicity Work

Synchronicities occur when your desire's vibration attracts cooperative vibrations, thanks to the Law of Attraction. Negative mindsets are also synchronistic events reflecting internal resistance. Recognizing synchronicity requires accepting interconnectedness, knowing the outer world is a mirror of your internal state, and that you can change it if you don't like what's happening.

Examples

- Meeting someone you were just thinking about: Have you ever been thinking about someone and then run into them unexpectedly? This is a common example of synchronicity.
- Seeing repeating numbers: Angel numbers are repeating numbers sent as messages from the Universe. You may see these numbers consistently in places like the time, phone numbers, addresses, or license plates. Discover the mystical world of Angel Numbers and fundamental Numerology in my other book, *The Spiritual Meanings of Numbers*, where you can unlock the secrets to calculating your Angel Numbers and gain a deeper understanding of these divine messages.
- Dreaming of a specific person, place, or thing and then encountering it in waking life: This could include dreaming of a certain location and then being unexpectedly invited to visit there or dreaming of a particular animal and then seeing it in real life.

PRACTICING THE LAW OF ATTRACTION

To use the Law of Attraction:

1. Focus on what you want and make detailed mental images of it as if it has already happened.
2. Visualize your desires, feel your beliefs deeply, practice gratitude, and maintain a positive mindset.
3. Avoid negative thoughts and beliefs.
4. Be patient and trust the process as the Universe works to bring your desires into reality.

The Law of Attraction is about manifesting what you want but not being selfish.

Practice Makes Perfect

Practicing the Law of Attraction daily can greatly impact your ability to manifest what you want. By trying new things and practicing until they become second nature, the possibilities for success are endless. While changing habits can be hard, staying optimistic and following proven tactics can help. It takes 21 days to create a new habit and 90 days to make a lifestyle change, whether it's exercise or manifesting.

Making Time

Practicing the Law of Attraction is easy once you know how to make the most of your time. Utilize every free minute from the moment you wake up until you go to bed. Set aside 2-5 minutes in the morning and at lunch, 10 minutes during your commute, and 5 minutes before bed. You can even practice while speaking. Here are some tips to improve your manifestation throughout the day, even during mundane tasks like commuting or waiting at the doctor's office:

Ways To Practice

Visualization

Start your day with a positive mindset by visualizing how you want your day to unfold. Then, spend two minutes imagining each hour of the day in a positive light, seeing and feeling yourself strong, happy, and achieving your goals.

Focus On Goals

To make a request from the Universe, write down your goals, big or small, to stay focused. Focus on things that add value to your life, such as meeting work targets or developing new skills.

Affirmations

To start your day positively, speak your affirmations out loud in front of the mirror before leaving the house. Keep it simple, like "Today will be a great day." You can also record and listen to them while commuting.

Read

Enhance your practice by reading relevant materials during your commute if taking transit, listen to audiobooks if driving. Choose books on specific goals or issues and take a step closer to achieving them by the time you reach your destination.

Meditate

Meditation can be a powerful tool for accessing your energy centers, including those in the gut, heart, and head. By quieting the mind, you can work on increasing the energy created below the navel, improving intuition and connection with your desires.

Guided Meditation

Sit comfortably, close your eyes, and reflect on any recurring patterns in your life. Notice any limiting beliefs or negative thoughts that may be contributing to these patterns. Identify lessons learned and apply them to activate the Law of Attraction for positive experiences in the future. Visualize healing energy filling and healing you from within and dissolve any unwanted patterns or beliefs. Finally, visualize what you want to manifest in detail, energize it with your breath, and sit for a few moments to notice any internal shifts and feelings before opening your eyes.

Be Kind to Yourself

Eat nutritious foods, have stimulating conversations with colleagues, do creative visualization during lunch, and perform random acts of kindness, like giving your seat to a stranger, holding the door for someone, or complimenting a colleague's achievement.

Spread Positive Energy

To foster a positive atmosphere, be a generator of positive vibes. Spread good news, steer clear of negativity, and motivate your loved ones with upbeat remarks and fresh ideas.

Reflect

Share your daily highlights with loved ones to reaffirm your progress and stay focused on attracting what you want. Remember that the Law of Attraction takes time, so stay persistent and optimistic.

Gratitude Journaling

End each day by writing in your gratitude journal to attract even better days in the future. Record things you're thankful for, big or small, like a work promotion or a laugh with friends. Then, before you go to sleep, make a habit of jotting down at least five positive things from your day. Doing so will allow these pleasant thoughts to permeate your mind as you rest, helping them seep into your subconscious.

ACTION STEPS

- To manifest your desires, take inspired action toward your goals, no matter how small.
- Set aside time each day to practice the Law of Attraction.
- Practice gratitude for what you already have and visualize more abundance coming to you.

- Spread positivity to those around you, including family, friends, and coworkers. Be the source of positive energy and good vibes.
- Surround yourself with people who uplift and inspire you, offering guidance and support in manifesting your desires.

UP NEXT:

Like the Law of Correspondence in the last chapter, the Law of Attraction emphasizes the power of our thoughts, feelings, and beliefs in shaping our reality. By becoming aware of our internal state and shifting our thoughts and emotions toward positive, aligned vibrations, we can create a corresponding external reality that reflects abundance, joy, and fulfillment.

The Law of Assumption, a complementary principle to the Law of Attraction, posits that our deeply held beliefs and assumptions are the true architects of our reality. When we wholeheartedly embrace the feeling of our desires and confidently assume their manifestation, we actively participate in the creation of our own lives, turning aspirations into tangible experiences.

When someone wants something and focuses their thoughts and emotions on that desire, they send vibrations into the Universe that attract similar vibrations back to them. This is the process of manifestation, where thoughts and desires are turned into tangible realities.

The Law of Attraction suggests that by focusing on positive thoughts and emotions, you can manifest your desires and attract positive experiences into your life. However, it is important to note that the Law of Attraction is not a quick fix, and working toward one's goals is also necessary for manifestation.

In the following chapter, we will delve into the Law of Inspired Action. This principle highlights the significance of taking action toward our goals with a sense of purpose and eagerness. It suggests that when we align our actions with our values and desires, we create momentum toward our aspirations and attract opportunities that aid our journey. By engaging in inspired action, you can surpass obstacles and achieve your goals with more satisfaction and fulfillment.

6

THE LAW OF INSPIRED ACTION

Manifestation without action is only a wish.

— NANETTE MATHEWS

INSPIRED TO ACHIEVE

There are times when I feel stuck and uncertain about how to proceed with my work. Recently, I was facing writer's block while working on a project. Even though I tried to keep going, I felt uninspired and lacked motivation.

Then, I remembered the Law of Inspired Action, which prompted me to take a break from writing and reflect on my values and desires. I spent some time journaling and thinking about what had initially inspired me to start writing. This exercise helped me regain my creativity and sense of purpose.

Feeling renewed, I decided to take a walk in nature and let my thoughts flow freely. As I strolled, ideas began to form, and I felt motivated to return to writing. So I sat back down at my desk and started typing with a level of enthusiasm and focus that I hadn't experienced in weeks.

By taking a step back and engaging in inspired action, I overcame my writer's block and made progress toward my goal. The Law of Inspired Action reminds us that when we align our actions with our values and desires, we can conquer obstacles and achieve our objectives with greater ease and satisfaction.

What Is Inspired Action?

Inspired Action emphasizes the importance of taking real, actionable steps toward achieving one's goals. This approach involves surrendering to the guidance of the Universe and listening to the inner voice within oneself. By following intuition and taking Inspired Action, individuals allow their dreams to manifest in unexpected ways. Trust in the Universe is at the heart of Inspired Action.

Action vs. Inspired Action

Action refers to taking steps toward your goals, such as going out to socialize or joining a club to meet new people. Inspired Action, on the other hand, refers to taking action that is guided by your intuition or inner knowing and feels right or aligned with your desires (Keithley, 2021). It's the action derived from a deep inner calling, even if it doesn't necessarily make logical sense. Only you can know if your actions are inspired; Inspired Action should feel good and like coming home. It often requires going outside of your comfort zone and releasing resistance to the guidance of the Universe.

Examples

An example of inspired action is when you take healthy risks that feel good and right to you on a deep level, even if it may not make logical sense or seem difficult initially. It's a decision or action that comes from a place of inner knowing and intuition rather than from external pressures or expectations.

Big

A person was working a well-paying job with colleagues they enjoyed being around, but their work was not fulfilling. Despite their fears of leaving a secure income, they felt a strong urge to pursue their passions and create a life that would excite them every day. After months of resistance, they shared their thoughts with their partner, family, and friends, who provided unwavering support. Then, with a leap of faith and surrender to the Universe's guidance, they discovered it was the best decision they had ever made.

Or Small

A smaller example of inspired action could be as simple as having a sudden urge to reach out to a friend or family member. Even if you don't understand why you feel this way, following through with it could lead to a meaningful conversation or an unexpected opportunity. Another example could be feeling the need to take a different route home from work and stumbling upon a new place to eat or a beautiful scenic route that you wouldn't have known about otherwise. Although these actions may seem small, they have the potential to bring positive outcomes and opportunities that you may not have experienced otherwise.

Journal Prompts

As you reflect on your own intuition, you may ask yourself whether you consider yourself to be intuitive and why or why not. Consider past experiences where you followed your intuition and made the right choice. On the other hand, think about times when you ignored your intuition and regretted it and what you can learn from those experiences. Finally, when making decisions, ask yourself whether you rely more on logic or intuition and whether you trust yourself to make good choices.

Take a moment to tune into your inner knowing and consider what it is telling you about your life right now. Are there any next steps you feel compelled to take, and how do you feel when you think about taking these steps? If you could take a single step this week that leads you closer to your dreams, contemplate what that step looks like and what your intuition is telling you about it.

Acknowledge that fear is a natural emotion that arises when taking a leap of faith and following your inner knowing. To help combat this fear, write at least ten affirmations about your strength, power, and courage to face the fear and move forward despite it.

Finally, ponder what inspired action means to you and whether it is worth taking, even if it may not always make sense.

WHEN TO TAKE INSPIRED ACTION

Knowing when to take Inspired Action is a personal decision that relies on intuition and self-connection, being open to guidance from the Universe, and taking risks outside of one's comfort zone.

One sign that it's time to take Inspired Action is a strong inner urge toward a particular goal or desire. This feeling can be persistent and difficult to ignore, becoming stronger as you move closer to your goal. Another indication is experiencing synchronicities or meaningful coincidences that align with your desired outcome. These can be unexpected events or encounters that point you toward the next step on your path.

Feeling enthusiastic and excited about taking action to reach a goal is another sign that it's time to take Inspired Action. This emotion fuels motivation and signals that your actions are aligned with your desired outcome. When moving toward your goal, an embodied sense of alignment or flow in life is another sign; it feels like everything is coming together, and the Universe is supporting your journey, resulting in ease and grace that can overcome any challenges.

Ultimately, deciding to take Inspired Action requires listening to intuition and being courageous enough to take healthy risks. Pay attention to the Universe's signs, take action when called to do so, and create a life aligned with your deepest desires and aspirations.

HOW TO TAKE INSPIRED ACTION

It is common to discover that taking Inspired Action does not come naturally to you, whether starting or continuing to explore manifestation. Trusting the Universe is a gradual process that requires self-reflection, trial and error, and patience. Some people may be naturally skilled at recognizing and responding to the Universe's signs, whereas others may require more time to develop this ability.

Living Now

To take Inspired Action, learn to live in the present moment. While planning is essential, having some flexibility is crucial. Set aside dedicated time each day to be present and do whatever feels right without questioning it. Learning to live in the now is an essential step toward taking Inspired Action and manifesting your desires.

Trust

Trust the manifestation process, even if you lack confidence. The ideas you receive are purposeful, so trust the outcome. Establish trust with the Universe, starting with small steps. Take small actions and see positive results to build your belief in Inspired Action. Start small, trust the process, and enhance your confidence.

Alignment With Desire

To take Inspired Action, you must be aligned with your desires and embody their energy. Without clarity and alignment, inspired action cannot come forth. Ask yourself how you would feel if you already had what you want, what kind of energy you would embody, and take action to embody that energy. This can be trying new hobbies, surrounding yourself with people who radiate that energy, or listening to certain music. These actions help you tune into the energy of your desire and fully embody it.

Signs and Synchronicities

After embodying the energy of your desire, paying attention to signs and synchronicities is important. This means being aware of how they may come to you without actively seeking them out. To notice these signs, you need to be present and mindful of your surroundings. Practicing mindfulness can help you avoid missing important messages meant to guide you toward your desires. If you would like to explore this topic further, I invite you to check out my books, *The Spiritual Meanings of Numbers* and *From The Universe With Love*.

Listen

To take inspired action, notice signs and messages, and trust in the Universe. Some action may challenge and push you out of your comfort zone, but it leads to desired results. Conversely, staying stagnant in your comfort zone guarantees no change.

Reflection

Revisiting past actions and experiences is crucial to manifesting your dream life. By taking action, you gather mental data on what works and what doesn't. Reflecting on your experiences with inspired action helps build trust in the Universe, making it easier to take bigger leaps in the future for significant results.

ACTION STEPS

- To take inspired action toward your goals, create a plan by breaking down the steps into small, manageable tasks.
- Write affirmations that empower and strengthen your inner spirit. These positive statements will give you the courage to overcome your fears and keep moving forward toward your goals.
- Surround yourself with supportive people who have achieved similar goals and can offer guidance.
- Use mindfulness and visualization techniques to align your thoughts and emotions with your desired outcomes.
- Quiet your mind and connect with your intuition.

UP NEXT:

The Law of Intuitive Action encourages us to trust our inner voice and follow our intuition, which can be difficult in a world that values logic above all else. By embracing this law, we can unlock our potential and achieve fulfillment in all aspects of our lives. Our intuition will guide us toward the path meant for us, even if it's unconventional or difficult.

This law invites us to take bold action toward our dreams, letting go of fear and doubt and having faith in the power of our intuition to guide us toward our purpose. Let us trust ourselves and embrace the Law of Intuitive Action, knowing it holds the key to leading us toward a life of joy, abundance, and fulfillment. The Law of Attraction sets the stage for manifestation by creating a strong intention and belief in what we want to achieve, while the Law of Inspired Action prompts us to take the necessary steps toward our goals with enthusiasm and determination.

Manifest your dreams beyond your wildest imagination by trusting your intuition and taking inspired action. Living in the present moment creates a powerful force that can bring our desires to life. Trust in the manifestation process and believe that the Universe is on our side, even when doubts and fears arise.

Experience profound joy, fulfillment, and abundance by overcoming obstacles and challenges that once seemed insurmountable. Witness the magic and wonder of seeing your dreams come to life by embracing the Law of Intuitive Action, taking bold steps, and trusting yourself and the Universe. Savor the journey, revel in the beauty of the present moment, and know that each step brings you closer to your deepest desires.

In the upcoming chapter, we will explore energy and the transformative power of the Law of Perpetual Transmutation of Energy. This law empowers us to shape our lives through our thoughts, beliefs, and actions, directing energy toward positive outcomes. By embracing this law, we can tap into our inner strength and courage to take bold actions toward our goals, trusting that the Universe is supporting us every step of the way. Furthermore, through energy transmutation, we can manifest our deepest desires, leading to a life that is abundant, fulfilling, and aligned with our true purpose.

Manifesting Your Reality: An Interlude

"Ask, Believe, Receive." - The Universe

From our initial exploration of the Universal Laws, we've delved deep into the foundational principles that shape our lives. This journey of discovery and enlightenment is the heartbeat of this book.

Our mission isn't just to understand; it's to share, grow, and light the way for others. And this is where you play a crucial role.

Every voice, every insight, holds the power to influence and inspire. Your unique experiences, your personal revelations, can be a guiding star for others on a similar journey.

By leaving a review for this book on Amazon, you're not merely offering feedback; you're providing a beacon for others to follow. By sharing your own connections with these laws and the transformations this book has spurred, you contribute to a larger narrative of growth and enlightenment.

Thank you for being such an essential part of this expedition. Always remember, in the vast expanse of the universe, every voice adds depth, dimension, and direction. Your voice truly matters; it's a beacon in the vastness of space.

7

THE LAW OF PERPETUAL TRANSMUTATION OF ENERGY

There's no matter here you can't re-matter into love.

— LAURIE PEREZ

TRANSFORMING ENERGY

The Law of Perpetual Transmutation empowers us to shape our lives by transforming negative energy into positive energy. Understanding and tapping into this Law enables us to manifest our desired reality through positive thoughts and intentions aligned with our goals. The Law's possibilities are limitless as it draws on the universal energy surrounding us. Healers, psychics, and truth seekers are familiar with the Law's power, using intention and positive energy to create healing and transformation (Kuna, n.d.). This is a reminder to us all that positive change is achievable no matter our circumstances.

About Manifestation

The Law of Perpetual Transmutation of Energy can be a powerful tool for manifestation. You can use this knowledge to direct your energy toward what you want to manifest by recognizing energy is always in motion. This means transforming your emotions into actions that will assist you in achieving your goals.

It is important to note that this Law applies to all forms of energy, including the thoughts and emotions that we hold within ourselves. Focusing on positive thoughts and emotions can raise our vibration and attract positive experiences into our lives. On the other hand, if we hold onto negative emotions without processing and releasing them, we risk storing unwanted energy within ourselves that can manifest as physical or emotional pain.

The Superpower Law

The Law of Perpetual Transmutation of Energy is a powerful Law that can help us manifest our deepest desires. It's like a superpower because it allows us to tap into the incredible power of energy and unlock a new level of potential, enabling us to achieve our greatest dreams. Knowing that energy is constantly in motion and can be transformed is key to directing it toward our goals. Armed with this knowledge, we can take control of our lives and create a sense of empowerment that can propel us toward positive change.

Non-Resistance

The Laws of Non-Resistance can help you transmute energy by teaching you to redirect your focus from negative thoughts and resistance toward positive outcomes. By understanding that what you resist persists, you can learn to let go of negative experiences and redirect your energy toward what you want to manifest. This can open up energy portals and attract success and positivity into your life. To use the Law of Non-Resistance effectively, it's important to discipline your mind to think positively and respond to situations instead of reacting.

EVERYTHING HAPPENS FOR A REASON

The concept of "everything happens for a reason" is often attributed to the belief in fate or destiny. However, it can also be viewed through a more practical lens. It means that every event or experience in our lives has a purpose, a lesson to be learned, and an opportunity for growth and improvement. By redirecting our focus from negative thoughts and resistance toward positive outcomes, we can transmute negative energy into positive energy and attract success and positivity into our lives.

Preparation

Everything happens for a reason, even the tragedies that seem outside of our control. It's all part of preparing us for a brighter future. Success cannot be achieved without experiencing the pain of defeat. But, even though it may not make sense at the time, once we move forward, we can see that these experiences have allowed us to grow and develop in ways we never thought possible.

Resilience

Failures, tragedies, and defeats can make you more resilient over time. Although it may be challenging to overcome the biggest heartbreaks, it's okay because they shape you into a stronger person, ready for what's to come. Remember that tough times don't last, but tough people do. Scars are a reminder of where you've been and what you've learned. Look how far you have come. Lift yourself up and appreciate the simple things in life. While you can't control everything, you can control how you react.

Old Beliefs

When we experience failures due to our own behavior, it can shatter our old beliefs and ego. Changing ingrained beliefs is hard, especially when we're comfortable in mediocrity. But breaking those old beliefs can be powerful; it opens up new ways of thinking and approaching life. We often fall into limiting behaviors because of our habits, chasing short-term pleasure and avoiding pain. But if we focus on long-term progress, we can make significant improvements over time.

Progress

Progress, not perfection, is key. Imagine improving just 1% of any area of your life each day. That 1% compounds over time, leading to massive growth. Unfortunately, we often remain stagnant until we experience pain or failure that forces us out of our comfort zones. But when that happens, we have a choice: fall backward or make progress. Use those moments of failure to propel yourself forward and keep making progress toward your goals.

Empathy and Authenticity

Empathy requires experiencing major defeat and tragedy, which allows us to truly relate to others who have gone through similar experiences. This kind of empathy makes you more authentic and less superficial, which is rare in today's world. Our true selves emerge when tragedy strikes, and we become more transparent and genuine.

TRAINING YOUR MIND: APPLICATIONS FOR MANIFESTATION

The power of your subconscious mind is incredible. It's where every thought is transformed into tangible reality. However, to fully tap into its potential, you must train your mind to align with your intentions. This is especially true when it comes to manifesting money.

Many of us have conflicting thoughts that can hold us back from achieving our goals. For example, you may consciously want to build a successful business and manifest abundance, but deep down, your subconscious doubts your ability to do so. These mixed messages and energies can create roadblocks on your journey to financial prosperity.

But don't let these doubts hold you back! With the right mindset and training, you can overcome any limiting beliefs and access the full potential of your subconscious mind. Start by visualizing your desired outcomes and believe in your ability to manifest your goals. Then, feel that belief deep within yourself. Train your subconscious mind by consistently feeding it positivity and reinforcing your belief in your abilities through techniques like positive affirmations, meditation, and mindfulness.

Negativity

Embrace the power within you to overcome any obstacle and create the life you desire. The Universe operates on the Law of Non-Resistance, which means that resistance only creates more resistance. This Law applies to both Karma and change—if you don't learn the lesson presented to you, you will continue to face similar challenges until you do.

It's easy to get stuck in negativity and focus on problems rather than solutions. But if you shift your mindset to one of problem-solving, you will attract positive outcomes into your life. Don't let fear or doubt hold you back from trying new things and taking risks.

Ego

There are plenty of ways to recognize when your ego is holding you back from experiencing the flow of energy and undergoing transformation. If you find yourself constantly complaining about every little thing that goes wrong in your life, it's a clear sign that your ego is in control.

To overcome this, it's essential to calm your ego and be true to yourself. When you act from a place of inspiration and authenticity, you tap into the power of your thoughts and achieve your goals. So, don't let your ego hold you back from living your best life!

Application In Your Life

Your subconscious mind is a powerful tool that can shape your reality. It's the place where thoughts and ideas turn into tangible manifestations. But, it's essential to recognize that limiting beliefs and mental blocks can interfere with this process, preventing you from achieving your desires.

Life is full of ups and downs, and it's impossible to control everything that happens to us. However, you have control over your mindset and how you react to situations. Focusing on positive events and what makes you happy will attract more of the same into your life. When you let go of negativity, you'll notice a shift toward positive experiences and outcomes.

It's crucial to align your goals with your moral values. Manifesting something that doesn't align with your values won't bring you true happiness or contentment. Practicing kindness and gratitude toward others and yourself will raise your vibrational energy, making it easier to attract positive experiences.

Meet Ben

Ben faced a challenging situation when he lost his job due to company downsizing. Initially disheartened, he transformed this setback into a valuable lesson for personal growth. Ben took the opportunity to explore his passions and skills, something he hadn't done in a while, and this period of self-reflection led him to discover a newfound love for entrepreneurship. Despite the challenges and uncertainties, he decided to start his own small business, developing resilience, determination, and adaptability along the way. As his company began to thrive, Ben found a deep sense of fulfillment he hadn't experienced in his previous job, demonstrating how adversity can lead to personal strength and growth.

Share It

The Universe is a boundless source of energy, constantly flowing and available to everyone. Remember this when you manifest abundance in your life. Once you receive what you desire, it's important to avoid the temptation to hold onto it or use it exclusively for yourself.

Wealth and money hold special meaning when it comes to sharing with others. You can share your wealth by utilizing services, supporting local businesses, donating to a charity, or generously tipping. These resources truly shine when used to bring happiness and contentment to both yourself and others. Therefore, cultivating the habit of sharing your abundance can lead to the Universe bestowing upon you even greater prosperity and happiness.

Conserve Sexual Energy

Harnessing your sexual energy can be a powerful tool for achieving success in all aspects of life. Some of the most successful and famous individuals in history, such as Nicola

Tesla, Steve Jobs, and Muhammad Ali, believed in the transmutation of sexual energy (Abundance No Limits, n.d.). They recognized that by controlling and directing this powerful force, they could use it to fuel their ambitions and achieve greatness.

Instead of allowing sexual energy to distract or diminish their focus, they channeled it into other areas of their lives, such as creative pursuits or physical fitness. This allowed them to tap into their full potential and achieve remarkable success.

ACTION STEPS

- Cultivate an attitude of gratitude by taking time to acknowledge and appreciate the abundance and blessings in your life. Show your appreciation through kind actions and gestures toward others.
- Embrace change as a positive aspect of growth and progress. Adapt and evolve with life, trusting your ability to handle challenges.
- Shift your energy from negative to positive by using positive affirmations and visualization techniques. This can help you release any blockages and attract positive experiences and people toward you.
- Surround yourself with experiences and individuals that align with your desired vibration and energy level. Cultivate positive emotions such as joy, love, and gratitude to attract more positivity into your life.
- Practice letting go of resistance and surrendering to what is. This means accepting and allowing things to

unfold as they are without trying to control or manipulate them.

UP NEXT:

Let us take inspiration from the Law of Perpetual Transmutation of Energy, a powerful concept that enables us to transform our lives and materialize our deepest desires. This Law explains converting negative energy into positive energy. Energy is never created or destroyed, only altered. The Universe is an abundant source of energy waiting to be transformed into positive experiences.

It is essential to remember that everything happens for a reason. Even tragedies and failures can prepare us for a brighter future. By converting negative energy into positive energy, we can become more resilient and empowered to face any challenge. The Law of Perpetual Transmutation of Energy gives us the power to unlock our inner potential and access the limitless possibilities of the Universe.

The Law of Inspired Action and the Law of Perpetual Transmutation of Energy are closely intertwined. The former emphasizes taking action that feels inspired and aligned with our goals, while the latter asserts that energy is always in motion and can be transformed to manifest positive experiences. In essence, inspired action activates the Law of Perpetual Transmutation of Energy and brings our manifestations to fruition.

Keep reading to learn how the Law of Cause and Effect teaches us that every action we take has a corresponding consequence.

It reminds us that we are the architects of our own lives and that our choices and decisions shape our future. By understanding this Law, we can take further control of our lives to manifest the reality we desire.

8

THE LAW OF CAUSE AND EFFECT

Shallow men believe in luck or circumstance. Strong men believe in cause and effect.

— RALPH WALDO EMERSON

ALL ACTIONS HAVE REACTIONS

The Law of Cause and Effect is a Law of the Universe that governs all actions and reactions. It asserts that every effect has a cause, and every cause produces an effect. According to the Law of Divine Oneness, our interconnectedness is such that every action we take has a ripple effect on the space around us, which in turn is connected to all other spaces in the infinite Universe. We must be aware of the energy we put out into the world because this Law reminds us that the motivations behind our actions matter. Being mindful of our actions and striving to generate positive energy can create a ripple effect of goodwill that benefits not only ourselves but also those around us.

ALL REACTIONS RETURN TO THE SOURCE

Every action in the Universe produces a reaction. This means every effect within our world has a cause, an original starting point. Every journey begins with a first step, and that initial action triggers a cascade of events with multiple outcomes that branch out in diverse directions. This Law applies to all aspects of the Universe, including human thoughts, behavior, and movements.

All thoughts lead to movements or human behavior, and all movements and behavior lead to further thoughts. A movement or action cannot occur without its original or preceding thought. According to this Law, there is nothing that happens by random chance. This is why the saying "We reap what we sow" is so important. For every action or thought, there is an equal and opposite reaction. Each action we take impacts everything we encounter, even the origin of the action itself. As a result, the effects of our actions will eventually find their way back to us in some shape or form.

Using the Law of Cause and Effect

In order to leverage the Law of Cause and Effect to our advantage, we must first define what significant change means for us and then establish the actions that will help us achieve it. This requires self-reflection, self-awareness, and taking account-ability for our lives.

Moreover, the Law of Cause and Effect teaches us that our reality mirrors the person we are and our convictions. Therefore, if we desire to create positive outcomes, we must concentrate on being the kind of person who exudes constructive energy into the world.

What Really Is "Good" or "Bad"?

The Universe is impartial and does not discriminate or judge us as deserving or undeserving (Brown, 2021d). It merely responds to the energy we emit, which is based on our beliefs and expectations.

Therefore, it's essential to cultivate positive and empowering beliefs about ourselves and our abilities. This may be difficult if we have limiting beliefs and negative self-talk. However, we can create a more fulfilling reality by being mindful of our thoughts and consistently working to shift our beliefs and expectations.

The Catalyst

To create a catalyst for success with the Law of Cause and Effect, take action toward your desired outcome by identifying necessary habits and committing to them consistently. For instance, to be a successful business person, you may need to create habits like waking up early, forming a morning routine, time blocking your schedule, and changing your conduct in the office. Remember that your present reality is a reflection of your past choices and self-perception. To change your reality, change your choices and self-perception.

Trauma

The Law of Cause and Effect states that your current reality results from the causes you've initiated in the past, and to change it, you must change your present causes. Trauma is a part of the macro system beyond our control, but we can control our response to it. So, instead of focusing on trauma, we can use the Law of Cause and Effect to make positive changes in our lives by intentionally selecting our thoughts, emotions, and behaviors. In addition, we can use our experience to help others who have been through similar events and focus on how we've overcome what we went through.

LAW OF CAUSE AND EFFECT VS. LAW OF ATTRACTION

The Law of Cause and Effect and the Law of Attraction are closely intertwined. The Law of Attraction suggests that we can bring positive experiences into our lives by focusing on positive thoughts, emotions, and feelings. On the other hand, the Law of Cause and Effect proposes an equal and opposite reaction for every action we take. Every action we take has a consequence or effect, and the Universe is in a constant state of balance. The concept of an equal and opposite reaction is rooted in the laws of physics and applies to both the physical and spiritual realms.

When you combine the two, you realize that thoughts, emotions, and actions are all causes that will result in corresponding effects. Therefore, you will initiate causes that bring about positive effects in your life if you intentionally choose positive thoughts, emotions, and behaviors.

AWARENESS

We need to have an understanding of our thought patterns since they have a significant impact on our reality. Our thoughts are responsible for creating our emotions and feelings, influencing our actions, and ultimately determining the outcomes we experience in life.

We become empowered to create the life we want by taking responsibility for our thoughts and actions—we can align our thoughts and actions with our desired outcomes, and by doing so, we can manifest positive experiences into our lives. Therefore, awareness of one's thought patterns is crucial for personal growth, self-improvement, and success.

KARMA

Karma represents the Law of Cause and Effect because it states that every action creates an equivalent response that comes back to the individual, sooner or later, in one form or another. The Law of Karma is impartial and universal, and no one can escape its effects.

The concept of Karma is not the same as fatalism. On the contrary, Karma ensures that individuals are personally responsible for their material and spiritual progress. Therefore, Karma is not a doctrine of distress but a harbinger of hope because one has the freedom to liberate oneself from past Karma by performing righteous actions in the right spirit (Singal, 2020).

Relationship Between the Law of Cause and Effect and Karma

The consequences of our actions may take varying amounts of time to come back to us—days, weeks, months, years, or even a lifetime. Like the Laws of the Universe, Karma has its own set of rules. By understanding them, we open ourselves up to new experiences, thoughts, and perspectives. We also gain the opportunity to generate more positive Karma.

The Great Law

Karma and the Law of Cause and Effect converge in the Great Law, which asserts that we attract the same kind of energy we radiate, regardless of whether it is positive or negative. This phenomenon applies even with strangers. Therefore, treat others kindly and with love, and they will treat you the same. Conversely, being condescending or disrespectful will result in the same treatment from others.

Creation

To make your dreams a reality, taking action is essential. The Law of Cause and Effect dictates that you must act to achieve your desires. Waiting passively will not bring your dreams to fruition. Inspirational figures like Oprah and Tony Robbins have succeeded by taking the initiative and creating opportunities that benefit others.

Humility

John McCloy once said, "Humility leads to strength and not to weakness" (Andary, 2021). This Law of Humility is embodied by many successful people who understand that acceptance of their current situation is necessary to create change. By resisting what we don't want, we give it power. Instead, focus on what you have and let go of what you don't want. Celebrate life and be aware of the good Karma you create.

Growth

To invite good Karma into your life, invest in personal development as per the Law of Growth. This doesn't only involve physical growth but also learning new skills, going back to school, volunteering, apprenticeship, reading, and more. The changes brought about by personal development can transform your external reality, including your environment. Growth can also involve shifting your mindset, letting go, forgiving, and healing from heartache, which can lead to positive effects.

Responsibility

The Law of Responsibility states that you are accountable for your life, including successes, failures, and overall development. Blaming others for your situation won't help you; you are the only one in control. Your mind is like a garden; you can cultivate it intelligently or let it run wild. The choice you make will determine the harvest (effect) you will receive, as positivity breeds positivity and negativity breeds negativity.

Connection

The Law of Connection teaches us that everything in the Universe is interconnected, and each step we take affects the outcome. This applies to our lives as well. Our past and present actions shape our future, and investing in positive behaviors and habits now will lead to good Karma later. We can create a fulfilling life by recognizing the links between our emotions and experiences.

Attention

The Law of Attention advises us to avoid overwhelming ourselves with multiple thoughts and tasks. Instead, break down goals into smaller tasks and prioritize them. By focusing on positivity and your highest values, you can avoid analysis paralysis and achieve more.

Kindness

The Law of Karma regarding giving and hospitality is clear: Be selfless and generous. This means sharing what you have with those in need and acting on your beliefs. Advocacy alone is not enough; you must also take action. If you support charity work, for example, don't just talk about it, but offer help to those who need it.

Moment

This Law, also called the Law of Forgiveness or the Law of the Present, encourages living in the moment and letting go of the past. Focusing on the past inhibits new thoughts and behaviors from forming. The future is shaped by your actions and thoughts today, so embrace the present to create a better future.

Transformation and Release

Albert Einstein once said, "Insanity is doing the same thing repeatedly and expecting different results" (Andary, 2021). Are you stuck in a pattern of repetitive experiences, such as attracting undesirable partners, difficult clients, or job rejections? If so, the Law of Change is sending a message that you need to evaluate your actions, behaviors, and habits to identify areas that require improvement.

Patience

This Karmic Law emphasizes that patience and consistent effort lead to eventual rewards, even if they don't come instantly. Hard work and persistence are key to achieving great things, and staying focused and celebrating each milestone along the way is essential.

Significance

The final Law of Karma affirms your inherent value and gifts. To make a positive impact on the world, use your unique abilities. The energy you project to the world will reflect back to you, so be mindful.

Attracting Good Karma

Here are some simple steps you can take to generate good Karma and positively impact the people in your life.

Love and Forgive—Yourself

Many struggle with low self-esteem, self-blame, and self-doubt, often dwelling on past regrets. To break free, focus on the positive aspects of your life and start each day with affirmations. As your mindset changes, your actions and relationships will also improve.

Love and Forgive—Others

Letting go of grudges is crucial for personal growth. Holding onto anger only hurts you. Forgiveness may be difficult, but it frees you from negative emotions and opens up space for positivity and good Karma in your life. When you forgive, two souls are set free.

Practice Kindness and Compassion

To attract good Karma, practice compassion and live by the Golden Rule, which teaches us to treat others as we would like to be treated. As Gandhi said, "Be the change you want to see" (LaMeaux, n.d.). This principle is not limited to one culture or religion but is a universal philosophy.

Reflect

To attract good Karma, reflect in quiet introspection. Explore your role in life events without judgment or blame, seeking understanding.

Practice

Consistency in attracting good Karma takes time. Practice kindness, compassion, self-love, and accountability for your actions to start sending and receiving good Karma daily. Hopefully, it will become a natural part of your life.

ACTION STEPS

- Assume accountability for your own thoughts and actions and aim to synchronize them with your intended results.
- Practice gratitude. The more you are grateful for things in life, the more things you attract to be grateful for.
- Embrace self-forgiveness and forgiveness toward others to release negative energy and move toward positivity.
- Examine your life and observe how your intentions, thoughts, and actions have contributed to your current experiences. Use this as an opportunity to make better choices in the future and witness the transformation of negative circumstances into positive ones.
- Employ visualization methods to imagine yourself taking positive steps toward your desired outcome, aiding in the manifestation of your aspirations.

UP NEXT:

Life is full of opportunities to impact the world around us positively, and the Law of Cause and Effect is a powerful reminder of this truth. Every thought, word, and action we take can create a ripple effect that has the potential to change the course of our lives and the lives of those around us.

The Law of Cause and Effect goes beyond just being a law of physics. It's a powerful reminder of the impact we can have on the world. It encourages us to be mindful of our actions and the energy we emit into the world. We must understand that even the smallest act of kindness can make a significant difference. We can manifest our desires and create the change we want to see in the world by taking responsibility for our lives and focusing on positive causes.

While the Law of Transmutation of Energy explains how energy is transformed from one form to another, the Law of Cause and Effect states that every action we take creates a certain amount of energy that will result in a consequence, which will be reflected back to us in some way. Together, these two laws suggest that everything we do, think, or say has a specific energetic consequence that will be transformed and redirected back to us by the Universe.

In the upcoming section, we will see how the Law of Compensation is a consequence of the Law of Cause and Effect. The energy that we generate through our actions, thoughts, and words will be transformed and redirected by the Law of Transmutation of Energy. This converted energy will produce a consequence that will be reflected back to us by the Universe. Remember, you are the master of your own fate, and the energy you put out into the world will ultimately determine the compensation you receive. So go out there and make every action count, every thought positive, and every word kind. The Universe will reward you accordingly.

9

THE LAW OF COMPENSATION

Spiritual growth involves giving up the stories of your past so the Universe can write a new one.

— MARIANNE WILLIAMSON

DIVINE RESTITUTION

The Law of Compensation reminds us that we will always receive in proportion to what we give. This Law operates in all areas of life, including our relationships, finances, and personal growth. The Universe responds by providing us with the resources and opportunities we need to succeed when we put in the effort and take action toward our goals.

Manifestation is also closely related to the Law of Compensation. By focusing our thoughts, feelings, and intentions on what we want to attract into our lives, we can access the vast resources of the Universe and align ourselves with the energy of success. When we visualize our desires with clarity and consistency, we send a signal to the Universe that we are ready to receive the compensation we deserve.

Remember, the Law of Compensation is not just about material gain. It's about leading a satisfying life and leaving a constructive influence on the world. When we give generously of our time, talent, and resources, we create a ripple effect of abundance that enriches our lives and the lives of those around us. So let us strive to live with purpose and intention and trust that the Universe will reward us in ways that exceed our wildest dreams.

THE UNIVERSE REWARDS YOU

This principle states that we receive in direct proportion to what we give. This means that every effort and contribution we make to the Universe will be rewarded—whether positively or negatively. It is closely related to the concept of Karma. Karma is the idea that our actions have consequences that affect our present and future lives. It's the belief that our thoughts, words, feelings, and deeds create an energy that comes back to us in a similar form. This means that if we do good, we'll receive good; if we do harm, we'll receive harm.

In essence, the Law of Compensation and Karma share the same fundamental principle: what you give is what you receive.

Both principles emphasize the importance of taking responsibility for our actions and being mindful of the energy we put out into the world. We can attract abundance, positivity, and good Karma into our lives by doing good and making positive contributions to the Universe.

How It Works

The origin of the Law of Compensation dates back to Ralph Waldo Emerson's publication of Essays in 184 (Manasa, 2021). In his essay, Compensation, Emerson described the world as a "mathematical equation" that must be balanced. It is an exact value and applies to everyone, emphasizing the importance of putting in the effort and taking responsibility for our actions to achieve positive results in life.

The Law of Compensation dictates there are no shortcuts in life. You receive in direct proportion to what you give, regardless of how much or little. If you put more effort into your relationships, career, and life, you will reap positive experiences as a reward. The reward may not come immediately or in the expected form, but you will eventually receive compensation for your efforts.

Aims

The Law of Compensation reminds us that every action we take has a corresponding reaction. It's not about profit or loss but about achieving balance and harmony in our lives. Like the ebb and flow of water, our lives are filled with ups and downs, and it's up to us to navigate these challenges with grace and positivity.

By embracing the dualism of life and taking responsibility for our actions, we can tap into the incredible power of the Law of Compensation. Whether we're making amends for mistakes we've made or reaping the rewards of our positive contributions, this Universal Law allows us to live with purpose and intention.

So strive to be mindful of the energy you put out into the world, knowing that every effort you make will be compensated for in some way, shape, or form. When we approach life with this awareness and a willingness to give our best, we can attract abundance, positivity, and success.

Difference Between Compensation and Attraction

The Law of Attraction teaches us that we have the power to manifest our desires into reality through our feelings, beliefs, and energy. However, simply thinking about something won't make it appear out of thin air. Instead, it requires proactive steps to bring it to fruition.

The Law of Attraction and the Law of Compensation go hand in hand. While the former emphasizes the act of receiving, the latter reminds us that we must give in order to receive. Therefore, we cannot simply take without putting in the effort to give back to the Universe.

Sir Isaac Newton's cosmic Law of action and reaction further reinforces this concept (Manasa, 2021). Every thought and action we take has a corresponding consequence, whether good or bad. By understanding and embracing the Law of Compensation, we can take deliberate and mindful action toward our goals, knowing that we will be compensated accordingly. Remember, the Universe is always in balance, and we have the power to attract abundance and positivity into our lives through our thoughts, feelings, actions, and energy.

Importance

The Law of Compensation is a powerful tool for personal growth and self-awareness. It reminds us of the impact that our thoughts and actions have on not only ourselves but also on others around us. By acknowledging this Law, we take responsibility for our mistakes and learn from them, making us better individuals. It is a valuable teaching tool that helps us to recognize the consequences of our decisions and motivates us to take positive actions in all aspects of our lives.

Personal

The Law of Compensation unveils duality in all aspects of life, serving as a tool to understand the impact of our thoughts and actions. By using this Law, we can achieve success and happiness through kindness to others, and the Universe will reward us. However, the Law also warns against harm to others, guiding our moral code and shaping our principles for a fulfilling and righteous existence.

Professional

Stay true to yourself and let the cosmic powers guide you to achieve success in your professional life. The Law of Compensation can be the key to unlocking better job opportunities, increased wealth, and the ability to build a successful business. Always strive to go above and beyond expectations and make it a habit no matter what kind of work you do. Doing so may reward you with greater wealth and stronger relationships with your employer or customers.

Make It Work for You

Here are five actionable steps to implement the Law of Compensation right away:

Affirmation

The Law of Compensation can be a powerful tool to attract positivity and abundance in your life, but it all starts with asking for what you want. Don't be afraid to dream big and affirm your desires into existence, as your thoughts and words have immense power in shaping your reality.

To truly harness the power of this Universal Law, it's important to retrain your subconscious mind and shift your focus toward positivity. Instead of making negative confessions, use affirmations to speak positive words and create a life filled with joy, love, and abundance.

Remember, the Universe constantly listens and responds to your energy and intentions. Therefore, by embracing the Law of Compensation and adopting a mindset of abundance, you can attract an abundance of blessings and experiences into your life.

Overcompensation

The secondary Law of Overcompensation is a strong second to the Law of Sowing and Reaping. By giving more than you expect to receive, you open yourself up to great rewards from the Universe. Going above and beyond what is expected of you can lead to greater compensation in the long run. To make this Law work for you, focus on giving without expecting anything in return. Shift your focus from what you will receive to what you can give, and trust that the Law of Compensation will take care of the rest.

Gratitude

It's vital to feel grateful and appreciate the blessings you already have so that you can attract more positivity and abundance into your life. When you focus on gratitude, you shift away from dissatisfaction and desires. When you fail to appreciate what you have, it's easy to fall into a cycle of lust and greed. Instead, be grateful for what you already possess rather than constantly craving more. Gratitude is a powerful tool that can help propel you forward in life. Although it can be challenging to remain grateful at all times, it's the foundation for increasing your overall happiness and success. By practicing gratitude, you can attract the things you desire most in life.

Abundance Mindset

An abundance mindset is the belief that sufficient resources are available for everyone to thrive. It allows you to recognize the endless possibilities within yourself and others. Embracing abundance leads to growth and development. Those who possess this mindset see that success is available to all. Rather than tearing others down, those with an abundance mindset root for everyone to succeed, knowing that there is plenty to go around.

Forgiveness

Your energy and attitude are crucial factors in determining your success. No matter how hard you work, negative emotions like anger and resentment will limit your rewards. The good news is that forgiveness can transform your attitude and improve your life.

By forgiving yourself and others, you can cultivate a positive attitude and inject love into your relationships and work. The Law of Compensation states that you must give before receiving, so choose to be the first to forgive, love, and show kindness. By doing so, you can inspire others to respond with love and compassion and create greater peace in your life.

Summary

Although the Law of Compensation may seem straightforward, it can be challenging to apply in real life—many people are accustomed to doing the bare minimum to get by. However, once you understand that what you receive is determined by what you give, your mindset can shift.

Instead of being solely focused on what you will gain, concentrate on what you can give. The Law of Compensation is not only about achieving financial success or a prosperous career. It's about recognizing the relationship between your contributions to the world and the rewards you receive in all aspects of life.

Once you begin to experience the incredible benefits of this Law, you will want to continue the cycle of giving and receiving. Like other Universal Laws, the Law of Compensation highlights the importance of taking action in your life and actively working toward your goals. Instead of waiting and hoping for things to happen, ask yourself what you can give to get what you desire (Manasa, 2021).

ACTION STEPS

- Assume responsibility for your thoughts and actions and align them with your desired outcomes.
- To release negativity and progress toward positive outcomes, practice forgiveness for yourself and others.
- Use visualization techniques to imagine yourself taking positive steps toward your goals, which can help you manifest them.
- Be generous and share your resources with others.
- Take consistent and purposeful action toward your goals. Set specific, realistic objectives and actively work toward them with determination and focus.
- Go above and beyond without expectation of anything in return.

UP NEXT:

The Law of Compensation teaches us that what we receive is directly proportional to what we give. This principle stresses the significance of taking responsibility for our actions, being mindful of the energy we emit into the world and living with intention and purpose. The Law of Cause and Effect is closely connected to the Law of Compensation since both laws revolve around the idea that every action has an equal consequence. The Law of Cause and Effect focuses on the broader concept of the interconnectedness of all things. In contrast, the Law of Compensation concentrates explicitly on the correlation between what we give and what we receive.

Essentially, the Law of Compensation is a particular instance of the Law of Cause and Effect. Both laws emphasize the importance of being mindful of our thoughts, words, and actions since they can potentially create positive or negative outcomes in our lives. By comprehending and applying these laws, we can take intentional and thoughtful steps toward achieving our goals, assuring that we will receive the consequences of our actions accordingly.

The next Law we will explain is the Law of Relativity, which holds an important key to manifestation. It reminds us that our experiences and perceptions are relative to our perspective. Therefore, when we face challenges or difficult situations, we can choose to view them as opportunities for growth and self-improvement rather than as obstacles that hold us back. By shifting our perspective and seeing challenges as opportunities, we can begin to manifest the outcomes we desire.

10

THE LAW OF RELATIVITY

Our life is what our thoughts make of it.

— MARCUS AURELIUS

SHIFTING REALITIES

Our unique viewpoints and experiences fundamentally shape our perception of reality. What may seem like a monumental challenge to one person could be a mere stepping stone for another, highlighting the significance of empathy and open-mindedness in comprehending the diverse perspectives that color our world.

RELATIVITY IN RELATIONSHIPS

A friend of mine was exhausted from dating the wrong people and feeling stuck and disappointed. So, they changed their perspective and decided to apply the Universal Law of Relativity to their dating life, viewing each date as an opportunity for self-discovery and growth.

My friend didn't feel a strong connection when they first went on a date with someone named Todd. However, they approached the date with an open mind and a desire to learn instead of feeling discouraged. To their amazement, Todd turned out to be one of the most fascinating individuals they had ever met, and my friend realized the value of learning from someone with a different perspective.

As my friend continued to apply the Law of Relativity to their dating life, they began to attract more positive experiences. Eventually, they met someone who was an excellent match for them. They recognized that by changing their mindset and seeing each experience as a chance for growth, they were able to manifest the love and relationship they truly desired. Therefore, my friend encourages others to do the same—shift their perspective, view each date as a chance for growth and self-discovery, and witness the influx of positive experiences in their lives.

EVERYTHING IS RELATIVE

Remember, manifestation is all about creating your reality through your thoughts, beliefs, and, most importantly, feelings.

When you view challenges as opportunities, you shift your mental processes, attitudes, and emotional responses from negative to positive, which can have a powerful effect on what you manifest in your life. With the Law of Relativity, you can choose to view difficult situations as temporary and within your power to overcome them. This perspective can help you stay focused on your goals and continue to manifest positive outcomes in your life. So, embrace the challenges that come your way, and use them as catalysts to create the reality you desire.

Law of Relativity

The Law of Relativity teaches us that challenges are opportunities for personal growth and character development. Without challenges, life would lack fulfillment and purpose. We must remember that our perspective shapes our experiences.

As we navigate through life, we will face challenges that test us and reveal areas where we need to grow. How we respond to these challenges determines our progress. For instance, repeating the same pattern in relationships may indicate a need to learn a lesson in self-love or setting boundaries.

By embracing the Law of Relativity and seeing challenges as opportunities for growth, we can create positive changes in our lives. So, when faced with a challenge, remember to trust the journey and use it as a chance to learn and grow.

Challenges

Life is a journey of growth and learning from our mistakes, embracing the challenges as opportunities to level up and raise our vibrations. The Law of Relativity, the most humanistic of all the Universal Laws, reminds us that everything negative is an opportunity. By shifting our perspective, we can become genuinely happy and optimistic, utilizing the lessons we learn to move forward with a higher vibration. Embrace the Law of Relativity and trust that every challenge is an opportunity to become the best version of yourself.

Perspective

The Law of Relativity challenges us to live with confidence instead of playing the victim. How we react to challenges shapes who we become, and when we dwell in the past and hold onto victimhood, we create a cycle of challenges.

I had a friend who embodied this victim narrative, and it held them back in life. They couldn't let it go and manifested more misfortune. While it is certainly possible to show others how to change, we cannot force anyone to do so. In light of this, it's crucial to prioritize our own self-care.

It taught me the importance of putting myself first and breaking patterns. I no longer try to fix others or their experiences, but I am here to help if they ask. Remember that it's okay to let go of relationships that aren't healthy for you. The Law of Relativity teaches us to embrace challenges and learn from them but also to prioritize our own well-being.

Takeaway Lesson

The Law of Relativity teaches us to approach life with a curious and open mindset. Even on tough days, we can honor our emotions and embrace curiosity to find lessons in challenges.

With each experience, we can grow and elevate to a higher frequency. Challenges push us out of our comfort zones and give us opportunities for transformation. Reflect on past "failures" to discover missed lessons. Challenges are opportunities to develop strength, empathy, understanding, and more. Approach every challenge with an open mind and willingness to learn and transform.

On Failures

The Law of Relativity teaches us that everything in life is relative, and that challenges and struggles are necessary for growth and progress. It also teaches us that failure doesn't actually exist in the way that we often perceive it. So, instead of viewing setbacks as failures, we can reframe them as opportunities to learn, grow, and move forward in a positive direction.

Avoiding failure may seem like a safe and comfortable option, but in reality, it can hold us back from achieving our full potential. By embracing failure and using it as a tool for growth, we can become more resilient, more confident, and more successful in every aspect of our lives. So don't be afraid to fail because, through failure, we can find success and fulfillment.

IT'S ALL ABOUT PERSPECTIVE

Stress can make us focus on the negative, causing us to miss out on the positive and lose balance in our lives. But gaining different perspectives can help us understand situations better and reduce conflict. By keeping things in perspective, we can evaluate what's truly important, let go of judgment, and react rationally rather than impulsively. Seeing both the strengths and weaknesses can help us be more objective and unbiased, leading to a more accurate understanding of where things stand. Remember, gaining different perspectives is key to maintaining balance and finding success in all areas of life.

Benefits

Gaining perspective offers numerous benefits that can improve our lives. It allows us to avoid being judgmental and have better relationships with others. It also helps to reduce stress and prevent impulsive reactions. We can develop greater empathy and connection by understanding others more deeply. Moreover, it provides clarity in our lives, allowing us to set goals and priorities that align with our values and aspirations. This leads to personal growth and learning opportunities, which enable us to navigate challenges and make informed decisions. Ultimately, gaining a clearer perspective can bring fulfillment and enrichment to our lives.

Growing Our Perspective: The Five Whys

The "Five Whys" method is a useful activity to balance our perspectives (Dandelion Training & Development, 2021). By repeatedly asking "why" about a simple or moderate problem, we can better understand its underlying causes and consider it from different perspectives. Thoughtfully considering each question helps us develop a clearer perspective and approach problems with a more open mind. With practice, we can find new viewpoints and navigate challenges more effectively.

Example

Problem: I am not manifesting the abundance that I desire.

Why is this happening? I am not consistently taking action toward my goals.

Why is that? I get easily distracted by other things.

Why is that? I am unsure of my priorities.

Why is that? I have not taken the time to reflect on what is truly important to me and the steps I need to take to get there.

Why is that? I have been focusing on seeking external validation and comparing myself to others rather than engaging in internal reflection and aligning with my values.

USING THE LAW OF RELATIVITY

You can make use of the Law of Relativity in different aspects of life. Here are five ways to apply it effectively:

Take Notice

To change your mindset:

1. Start by being aware of your thoughts.
2. Analyze everything you encounter and examine how you relate to it.
3. Remember, your perception is influenced by comparison.
4. Identify your relativity anchors and replace negative thoughts with positive ones to unlock a world of

endless possibilities.

Changing your thinking can transform your life for the better!

Relate Differently

Transform the relationships you create in your mind by challenging your perceptions. Ask yourself why you think a certain way and try to see things from a different perspective. Embrace your power to shift your perspective and reframe negative situations in a positive light. This ability can lead to a more fulfilling and satisfying life.

Think Big

Challenge your thoughts with wild comparisons to transform your mindset. Imagine being in the sun when it's too hot or appreciating not living in Antarctica when it's cool. Instead of dwelling on a low salary, be grateful for what you have. These comparisons shift your perspective and bring positivity to your life. Appreciate what you have, see the world differently, and cultivate a positive mindset for a happier life. When we shift our attention to what we already have and express gratitude for it, the Universe takes notice and responds with more of the same.

Be Grateful

Gratitude can be difficult to practice in tough times. But remember, your mind often creates your "hard place" by comparing it to something better. To cultivate gratitude, use the Law of Relativity to your advantage. For instance, if you're trying to lose weight, be grateful for the weight you're at. The ultimate gratitude is for being alive, as nothing compares to it. Take a moment to put things into perspective, and you'll realize how blessed you are—feel it. Remember, a positive mindset rooted in gratitude can transform your life.

Peel Labels

Break free from labels that contribute to your relative mindset. Instead of focusing on limitations, see the possibilities. Remember that nothing is until it is, and you have the power to create your reality. So, embrace your potential and live limitlessly.

ACTION STEPS

- Empower yourself with positive affirmations and visualization techniques to cultivate a mindset of strength and positivity, regardless of the situation.
- Employ the Five Whys to shift your perspective.
- Practice gratitude by finding the silver lining in challenging situations and embrace the opportunities for growth and learning they provide.
- Surround yourself with supportive individuals who motivate and encourage you, offering fresh perspectives and insight. Remember that you can conquer any obstacle and achieve your goals with the right mindset and support system.
- Notice which labels you apply to yourself and others and be mindful of the limitations they carry.

UP NEXT:

In conclusion, the Law of Relativity reminds us that everything in life is interconnected and that our thoughts and beliefs shape our reality. We can manifest our desired reality by embracing this Law and viewing challenges as opportunities for growth and learning. When we focus on positive outcomes and visualize ourselves overcoming obstacles, we attract positive energy and opportunities into our lives. By maintaining a positive mindset and aligning our thoughts, beliefs, and actions with our goals, we can create the reality we want to experience. Remember, the power of manifestation lies within us, and every challenge is an opportunity to strengthen our manifestation muscles and attract the life we truly desire.

While the Law of Compensation states that we will be compensated in proportion to the service we provide, the Law of Relativity states that everything in life is relative and that challenges and struggles are necessary for growth and progress. Next, we will explore how the Law of Polarity states that everything in the Universe has a polar opposite and that these opposites are two extremes of the same thing. Everything has a duality—light and dark, hot and cold, good and bad, and so on. Understanding the Law of Polarity can help us recognize that even negative experiences have positive aspects and that by focusing on the positive, we can attract more positivity into our lives. This is closely connected to the concept of manifestation, as the Law of Polarity teaches us that by focusing on what we desire rather than what we don't want, we can attract more of what we want into our lives.

11

THE LAW OF POLARITY

But there is no energy unless there is a tension of opposites.

— C.G. JUNG

POLAR OPPOSITES

Have you ever thought about how everything in life has a duality to it? For example, how would you know what heat is if you didn't experience cold? How would you know the feeling of joy if you didn't ever feel sadness? The Law of Polarity teaches us that everything has two sides, and we can't fully understand one side without experiencing the other.

When we want to manifest something, it's important to acknowledge that there may be contrasting experiences along the way. We may have to face challenges or obstacles before we can achieve our desired outcome. But by recognizing the duality in everything, we can maintain a balanced perspective and use those contrasting experiences as opportunities for growth and learning. We can learn to appreciate the journey, even when it's not all sunshine and rainbows.

THE LAW OF POLARITY: THE BEAUTY OF CONTRAST

There is a duality in everything, and everything has an opposite. This duality is necessary for our growth and expansion. We wouldn't be able to fully appreciate the good times without contrast, nor would we learn the valuable lessons that come with the difficult times. Contrast helps us manifest the reality we desire and allows us to experience and appreciate life in all its forms.

In the end, we come to realize that there is no good or bad; there is only contrast. Therefore, by embracing the Law of Polarity, we can learn to appreciate and find beauty in all experiences.

The Law of Polarity explains the existence of opposing forces or dualities in our world. It posits that everything has an opposite and that these opposites are forever linked together. By embracing this Law, we can view every situation as an opportunity for growth and learning. It encourages us to see the world in a different light.

Lessons

The Law of Polarity centers around the idea of opposites, contrast, and duality. Here are some of the greatest lessons to be learned from the Law of Polarity.

Appreciate the Good

Every moment of pain and sickness can teach us to appreciate the aspects of our lives we might otherwise take for granted. It's one of the greatest miracles of the Law of Polarity. Even the not-so-great experiences can lead to greater appreciation and gratitude for the good ones that come along.

When we face rejection or struggle with money, we can still find purpose and value in those experiences. It's up to us to choose our mindset and see every experience as an opportunity for growth and gratitude.

Value of Negative

One of the greatest lessons of the Law of Polarity is that everything has a purpose and value, even the things we may initially label as "bad." Take, for example, darkness and light. Symbolically, we often view light as "good" and darkness as "bad," but in reality, both have their own unique benefits.

We all carry shadows within us, but by embracing them and stepping into our darkness, we can uncover our innermost thoughts and feelings and use them to grow and transform. And just like darkness is beneficial for the health of the planet and our own biological health, our shadows are beneficial for our emotional and spiritual well-being.

What You Don't Want

Life is a journey of self-discovery, and our experiences, whether good or bad, serve as valuable lessons that help us grow and become better versions of ourselves. Every relationship, even the ones that don't work out, offers an opportunity to learn more about ourselves and what we truly desire. At the beginning of our dating lives, we may not have a clear idea of what we want in a partner, and that's okay.

It's easy to label our failed relationships as mistakes, but in reality, nothing is truly a mistake. Instead, every experience provides an opportunity to learn and grow. For instance, perhaps you never considered political views an important factor in a relationship until you dated someone with completely opposite views. This experience may have helped you realize that shared values are essential for a healthy and fulfilling relationship.

Examples

The Law of Polarity can be a helpful tool for change. Because this Law tells us that there's a duality in everything, and we can switch our thinking from negative to positive. Identify what the negative situation is teaching you, detach yourself, and ask what the positive alternative might be. For example, if you're lonely, what is this negative polarity teaching you? Now, take what you've learned and think about the steps you might need to take to change the negative situation. Remember, the simplest approach to change can often be the most helpful.

For example, a negative polarity is, "I don't have a significant person in my life to love," which can be reframed into "I have no one to love because I don't love myself right now" (Coster, 2019). This positive polarity suggests that the person needs to take more care of themselves and have pride in how they look and behave and make themselves available by being visible on dating services or joining some groups. One reason someone may feel lonely is that they are not exposing themselves to situations where they can potentially meet new people.

Building on that, consider Tom, who had always felt isolated and believed he lacked meaningful connections. Instead of focusing on the negative polarity of "No one wants to be my friend," he reframed his thinking to, "I haven't found my tribe because I've been avoiding social situations out of fear." Recognizing this positive polarity, Tom decided to challenge his comfort zones. He started attending local hobby groups and workshops, not only broadening his horizons but also gradually forging genuine friendships. This proactive shift underscored the importance of self-awareness and the proactive steps one can take when the underlying reasons for a situation are understood.

Questions to Ask

In what ways have you experienced contrast in romantic relationships? What you wanted versus what you didn't want. How about in your career? What did you want versus what you didn't want? Can you think of other examples of contrast in your life?

Can you recall a time when you experienced something you didn't want, and it helped you learn what you did want? How about a time when something went wrong, and it helped you appreciate when things were going right? For instance, did a bout of sickness make you appreciate your healthy body more, or did a broken appliance make you realize how important it was? Have you ever labeled something as bad, only to discover its value and meaning later?

Think about one aspect of your life that you wish you could change. What is it teaching you, and how can you grow through this experience? On the other hand, what's going really well in your life right now? Has it always been this way, or did past experiences teach you valuable lessons that led you to this point? For example, if you're in a great relationship or career, did past relationships or jobs help you realize what you didn't want, ultimately leading you to this positive situation?

MANIFESTATION AND THE LAW OF POLARITY

The Law of Polarity states that everything has two opposite poles, and this applies to our thoughts when manifesting. We may unintentionally attract the negative side if we focus on abundance but don't believe we deserve it. To strengthen our intent, we can visualize our future selves and feel it as though it has already happened. Ultimately, we must work on our core beliefs to manifest our desires.

Exercise

Draw a line down the center of a page and list what you want to manifest on the left and its opposite on the right. For each item, imagine having both the positive and negative versions and note which feels more achievable. If the negative resonates more, you have limiting beliefs to address. Remember, while your intentions may be in the right direction (left column), your energy may not align (right column).

ACTION STEPS

- To manifest your desires and shift your energy toward positivity, use positive affirmations and visualization exercises to replace negative thought patterns and beliefs with empowering ones.
- Surround yourself with positive influences, such as uplifting books, podcasts, and people who inspire you. This can help reinforce your positive beliefs and thought patterns and counteract any negative influences that may be holding you back.
- Practice mindfulness and observe your thoughts and emotions without judgment, focusing on finding balance and harmony.
- Cultivate a sense of acceptance and openness toward the polarities in your life, recognizing that they are part of the natural ebb and flow of the Universe.
- Take action toward your goals, even if they feel uncomfortable or scary. You can build confidence and momentum toward manifesting your desires by facing

your fears and taking steps toward what you want. Sometimes facing challenges can help us appreciate the positive more fully.

UP NEXT:

In conclusion, the Law of Polarity reminds us that even during the toughest of times, there's always a glimmer of hope that can light our path. This Law teaches us to embrace life's contrasts, recognize the value in both positive and negative experiences, and use them as catalysts for personal growth and transformation. We can transcend our limitations and tap into our full potential by embracing this principle, unlocking a Universe of possibilities we never thought possible. Remember that every obstacle we encounter is a chance to learn and grow. Every setback presents an opportunity to soar even higher.

The relationship between the Universal Law of Relativity and the Law of Polarity lies in their shared emphasis on interconnectedness and the many perspectives of any given situation. When we apply these principles to manifestation, we can understand that everything in our reality is relative to our thoughts, beliefs, and feelings and that our perspective can significantly influence our experiences. Furthermore, the Law of Polarity reminds us that there are always opportunities for growth and learning, even in difficult situations. By recognizing the interconnectedness of all things, we can develop a more balanced perspective and attract positive experiences into our lives. By understanding and embracing these Universal

Laws, we can manifest the reality we desire and unlock our true potential.

In our penultimate chapter of this book, we will examine how the Law of Rhythm is a powerful reminder that life is not a static and unchanging entity but a dynamic and ever-evolving force. Just as the tides of the ocean rise and fall and the seasons of the year shift from one to the next, we, too, experience cycles of growth and contraction in our lives. By understanding and embracing this natural ebb and flow, we can gain a sense of peace and confidence in our ability to weather any storm.

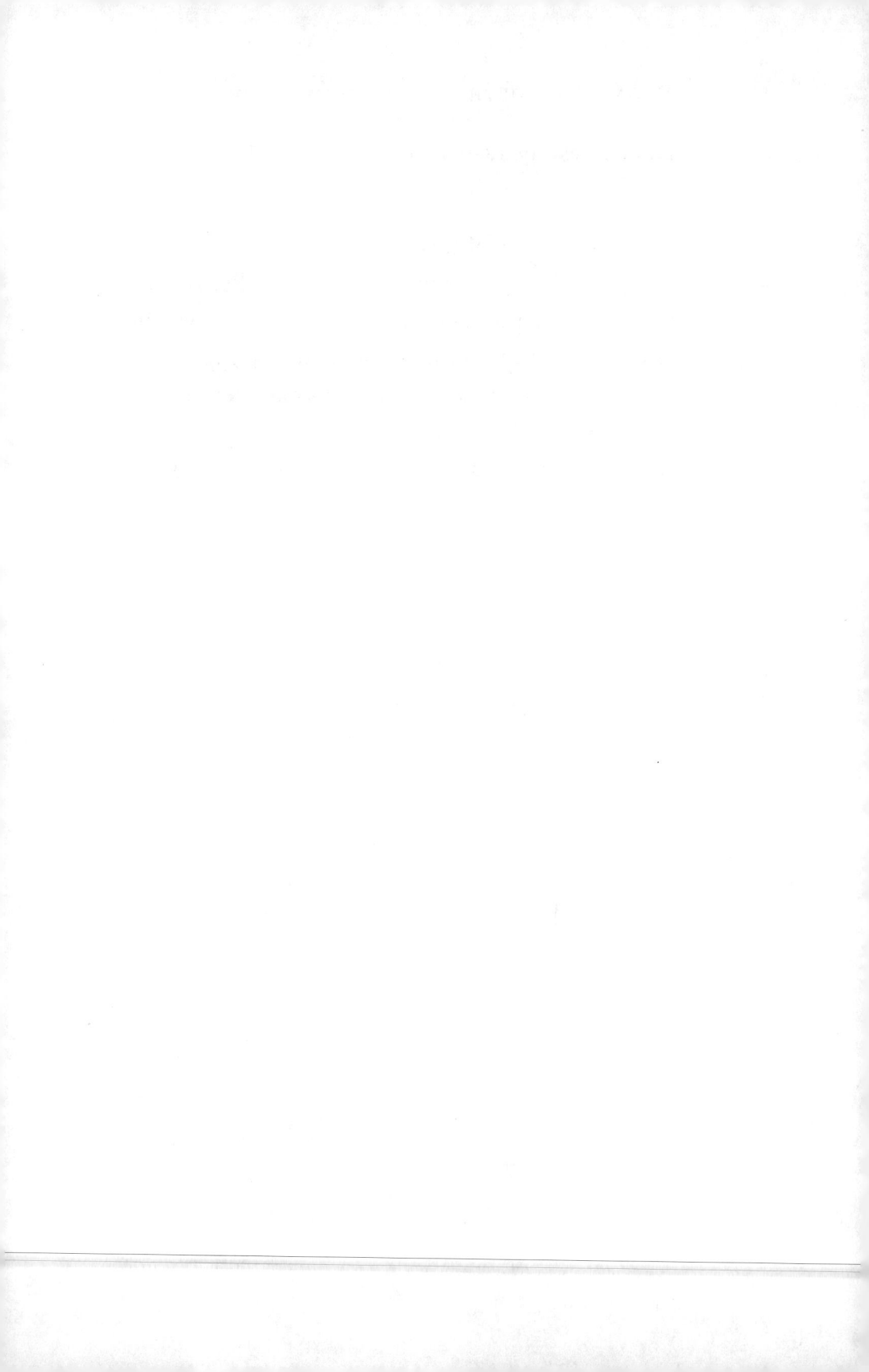

THE LAW OF RHYTHM

Nothing stands still—everything is being born, growing, dying—the very instant a thing reaches its height, it begins to decline—the Law of Rhythm is in constant operations...

— THREE INITIATES

FINANCIAL U-TURN

At times, it can be disheartening to struggle with finances. It feels like no matter how much effort is exerted; it never seems to be enough. This is where the Universal Law of Rhythm comes in, as it reminds us that our finances are subject to cycles of growth and contraction.

As I delved deeper into this Law and applied the other Laws we've discussed, I realized that my financial struggles were simply a natural part of life's ebb and flow. So instead of feeling defeated, I chose to embrace these cycles of growth and contraction in my finances.

Rather than dwelling on my setbacks, I took action by cutting back on expenses, increasing my income, and saving for the future. I was determined to take control of my financial future and not let it control me.

I began to see real progress as I persevered. My debts began to shrink, and my savings started to grow. I no longer felt trapped by my financial struggles but empowered to create the financial future I desired.

The Law of Rhythm enlightened me that financial difficulties are not a fixed condition but rather a phase that can be transformed over time. I found the courage to take action, which made the difference in turning my financial situation around.

THE PENDULUM SWING

The Law of Rhythm is like a pendulum swing, involving cycles of growth and contraction that resemble the back-and-forth motion of a pendulum (Chapman, n.d.-b). It reminds us that balance is key to flowing with life's cycles and patterns, a natural part of the Universe's movement and flow. By embracing this ebb and flow, we can strive to find our own center and create balance and harmony in our lives, helping us weather challenges and appreciate moments of joy and abundance.

Nothing Is Permanent

Nothing in life is permanent. Everything is subject to change, growth, and decay. The natural cycles and patterns of the Universe ensure that everything is in a constant state of motion. We see this in the natural world around us, from the changing seasons to the ebb and flow of the tides. The same is true for human endeavors, whether it's the rise and fall of civilizations or the fluctuations of the stock market.

By understanding that everything is impermanent, we can learn to embrace change and appreciate the moments of joy and abundance that come our way. We can also find comfort in knowing that the difficult times we face are temporary and will eventually pass. This realization can help us let go of attachment and find a sense of peace and acceptance in the present moment.

Rhythm Is Everywhere

The Law of Rhythm reminds us that everything in life moves in cycles and patterns. From the movements of the planets and the changing of the seasons to the fluctuations of the stock market and our own emotions, rhythm is everywhere. We often get attached to specific phases that make us feel good, but this Law teaches us to take a step back and see the bigger picture. We need all the phases, the ups and the downs, to create a holistic view of life. By embracing this Law, we can cultivate patience and trust in the process, knowing that nothing is permanent, and everything has its time. This mindset can help us find gratitude and appreciation for the present moment, regardless of its phase in the cycle.

Why Is the Law of Rhythm Important

The Law of Rhythm reminds us that life is full of cycles and patterns, both good and bad. By understanding and accepting this Law, we can learn to ride the waves of life instead of fighting against them. This can help us find balance and harmony in our lives, even during challenging times.

It's important to remember that nothing is permanent and that there is always an up after a down. By embracing the Law of Rhythm, we can cultivate a mindset of gratitude and keep pushing forward, knowing that the pendulum of life will swing back in our favor. This can help us navigate difficult times and appreciate the moments of joy and abundance that come our way.

GO WITH THE FLOW: MAINTAINING RHYTHM

Here are some suggestions for effectively following the Law of Rhythm:

- Observe thoughts: When life feels like it's happening to us, asking, "How am I feeling?" and "What do I need to do right now?" can help during lows. We have choices and opportunities in adversity. Use negative experiences for growth and self-improvement.

- Non-attachment: Aim for neutrality or indifference instead of attachment to outcomes. Non-attachment is crucial for emotional control during highs and lows. Detaching from expectations can prevent shock or disappointment during unfavorable outcomes, even in challenging periods.
- Embrace ebb and flow: True happiness doesn't depend on external circumstances beyond your control. By controlling your emotions, you can remain balanced when the tides turn. Embrace life's rhythms and patterns, including the ups and downs. Stay calm, be patient, and use your willpower to stay positive.

THE LAW OF RHYTHM AND MANIFESTATION

The Law of Rhythm teaches us to appreciate the different phases of life and maintain a positive outlook, even during difficult times. This Law assures us that our circumstances are constantly changing and will eventually return to a more desirable state. It is similar to the Law of Relativity, which reminds us to stay strong during challenges because better things are on the way.

While some may view this Law as pessimistic, it simply guarantees change, not necessarily bad outcomes. It encourages us to embrace the different phases of life, including changes in emotions, actions, thoughts, priorities, and relationships, which can ultimately lead to balance and wellness. Ignoring this Law can lead to burnout and stress, as we may try to force ourselves to remain productive when we need rest. Remember, even motivation is cyclical, so it's important to honor the natural rhythms of life.

Bad Experiences

The Law of Rhythm reminds us that our manifestation journey is a journey of ups and downs, with both positive and negative experiences. Don't let challenging situations discourage you—they can be the very thing that propels you forward and helps you grow. Remember, down cycles are normal and don't define your worth or ability to manifest what you desire. Every negative experience is balanced out by a positive one, and all phases bring new growth and opportunities. Embrace change, and all that life has to offer to maintain balance and wellness. To stay in sync with this Law, ask yourself if you victimize or blame yourself when things don't go as planned. Instead, accept obstacles as temporary and appreciate challenges, knowing that good experiences are coming. Even small changes in perspective can lead to significant improvements in emotional regulation, so keep an open mind and a positive outlook. Believe in yourself, trust in the journey, and watch as you manifest all you desire.

ACTION STEPS

- Visualize yourself flowing effortlessly with your life's natural rhythms and cycles, using them to propel you toward your goals.
- Become more present and aware of the current moment by practicing mindfulness. This heightened awareness can assist you in recognizing the rhythms

and cycles of your life and how they influence your thoughts, emotions, and behavior.

- Be self-aware and observe your own energy and emotions, allowing them to guide your actions and decisions.
- Reflect on past experiences and identify how they have contributed to your growth and development. This can help you develop a sense of gratitude and appreciation for the ups and downs of life and trust that everything happens for a reason.
- Trust and surrender to the natural cycles of the Universe, knowing that they are leading you toward your ultimate good.

UP NEXT:

The Law of Rhythm serves as a profound reminder that life moves in cycles and patterns, and we can harness its power to achieve our full potential. Instead of feeling overwhelmed by the ups and downs of life, we can use this Law to our advantage, learning to navigate the ebbs and flows with grace and ease. By recognizing that change is the only constant and nothing lasts forever, we can summon the strength and resilience to face challenges head-on and seize opportunities as they arise.

This Law encourages us to appreciate every moment, whether we are in a time of abundance or struggle. With gratitude and appreciation for the present moment, we can cultivate a mindset of positivity and trust that challenging times will eventually pass. We can find true happiness and fulfillment by practicing patience, non-attachment, and a willingness to adapt to life's rhythms.

Therefore, let us not resist the natural rhythms of life but rather embrace them, for they can lead us to our greatest moments of growth and transformation. By trusting in the Universe and maintaining a positive outlook, we can create the future we desire and reach our highest potential. Let us ride the waves of life with joy and confidence, knowing that every moment is an opportunity for growth and greatness that lies ahead.

The Law of Polarity, which we covered in the last chapter, and the Law of Rhythm are closely related because they both emphasize the importance of balance and harmony in the Universe. The Law of Polarity reminds us that polarities are necessary for balance, while the Law of Rhythm reminds us that everything is constantly in motion and that change is a natural part of life. Similarly, in the final section of this empowering book, you'll discover the profound wisdom of the Law of gender, which teaches us the importance of cultivating a harmonious balance between the feminine and masculine energies within ourselves. By embracing both aspects of our nature, we can tap into a limitless well of creativity, intuition, and strength, unlocking our full potential and achieving our dreams. So, get ready to embark on a journey of self-discovery and transformation as you learn to harness the power of this Law and unleash your true inner strengths.

THE LAW OF GENDER

Male and female represent the two sides of the great radical dualism. But in fact, they are perpetually passing into one another.

— MARGARET FULLER

GENDER LIBERATION

Welcome to the empowering world of the Law of Gender, where we discover the secret to unlocking our full potential through the harmonization of our feminine and masculine energies. This Law reminds us that both aspects of our nature are essential in manifesting our dreams and desires. By tapping into our creative and intuitive feminine energy and balancing it with our focused and driven masculine energy, we can manifest our greatest aspirations with ease and grace.

BEING AND DOING

The Law of Gender is a powerful reminder that we all possess feminine and masculine energies, regardless of gender. Like the Yin and the Yang, these energies are complementary and necessary for manifestation. And just as nature requires a balance of both energies to thrive, so do we.

In a society that has long prioritized masculine energy, it's important to acknowledge and tap into our feminine energy as well. This means embracing qualities such as empathy, intuition, and nurturing, which are often undervalued but essential for success and fulfillment.

The Law of Gender isn't about conforming to traditional gender roles but about finding a balance between two opposing energies that are both vital for our well-being. By embracing both aspects of ourselves, we can achieve a greater sense of wholeness and tap into our true potential. So, let's explore the nuances of masculine and feminine energy and discover how we can use them to manifest our deepest desires and live our best lives.

Masculine/Feminine:

Masculine

Masculine energy is a powerful force that drives action, logic, and willpower. It is the energy of focus, clarity, and goal-setting which makes it essential for achieving our loftiest aspirations. If you are naturally inclined toward leadership, problem-solving, and taking charge during crises, you are likely healthily tapping into your masculine energy. On the other hand, if you find yourself constantly busy, unable to slow down or rest, and striving for perfectionism in every aspect of your life, you may be leaning too heavily on your masculine energy.

Feminine

Feminine energy is a beautiful force of intuition, creativity, and empathy that allows us to forge meaningful connections with others. If you feel in touch with your inner wisdom and comfortable with your introverted nature, you're likely healthily harnessing your feminine energy. When you're at your most powerful, you radiate a sense of safety and vulnerability that draws people to you, making them feel seen and heard. However, if you're feeling stuck, unmotivated, or disconnected, you may need to tap into your feminine energy more.

CULTIVATING MASCULINE AND FEMININE ENERGIES

Here are some suggestions for cultivating your feminine energy:

- Meditate: Elevate your daily routine with a 10-20 minute meditation. Give your intellect a break and connect with your body, intuition, and natural presence.

- Dance: Get your mind and body in sync with the power of movement! Dance, stretch, or take a lighthearted stroll to create fluidity and shake things up.
- Chill: Indulge in some much-needed self-care by taking a bubble bath, sipping your favorite tea, and listening to soft music. Create a peaceful atmosphere by lighting candles and allow yourself to fully relax and be present in the moment.
- Create: Let your creativity flow! Don't worry about perfection or the final outcome. Take out your paints, clay, or any medium you like, and lose yourself in the joy of expressing your creativity.
- Nature: Spending time in nature can help us find a balance between doing and being. Take a hike, visit a park, and let yourself relax with the sights, smells, and sounds around you. Feel the grounding energy of trees and soak up the sun's warmth on your skin. Bring some plants or flowers into your living or work space and take moments to appreciate their beauty and positive energy.
- Share: Vulnerability begins with sharing. Open your heart and get real; you'll connect more deeply with yourself and those around you.
- Flow: Embrace the beauty of free-flowing days! Choose a day where you have no set plans and allow yourself to wake up and follow your intuition. Without any pressure to plan ahead, let your body lead you to the next activity that feels right.
- Relieve stress: To tap into our feminine energy and reduce stress, it's important to practice mindfulness.

Mindfulness allows us to connect with our intuition and creativity and break free from the grip of anxiety.

- Consider these recommendations for developing your masculine energy:
- Assert yourself: Speak up and share your opinions, wants, and needs with others. Don't be afraid to take charge and assert yourself in both personal and professional settings.
- Pursue adventure: Step out of your comfort zone and take on new challenges. Whether trying a new hobby or exploring a new city, seeking adventure can help you tap into your masculine energy.
- Set boundaries: Don't let others walk all over you. Set healthy boundaries with friends, family, and colleagues to ensure that you are taking care of yourself and your needs.
- Take healthy risks: Embrace the unknown and take calculated risks that align with your goals and aspirations. This could mean starting a new business, making a big career move, or asking someone out on a date.
- Connect with your body: Engage in physical activity and connect with your body to harness your masculine energy. Whether it's weightlifting, martial arts, or simply going for a run, physical activity can help you feel grounded and confident in your body.

BALANCING FEMININE AND MASCULINE ENERGIES

You don't need to take specific actions to "use" the Law of Gender. Instead, you need to develop an awareness of the energies surrounding you— this means paying attention to the masculine and feminine energies within yourself, your interactions with others, and your environment.

As you become more aware of the Law of Gender, you will notice patterns in your relationships and become more attuned to the world's natural rhythms. By cultivating a deeper understanding of yourself and the world, you will develop a greater sense of harmony and balance in your life. Ultimately, embracing the Law of Gender will allow you to live in alignment with the universal energies that govern our world.

There are four divine energy types:

Greater Yin

This embodies pure femininity—characterized by stillness, the night-time, intuition, creativity, emotions, and senses. You're highly sensitive and empathetic, feeling deeply and often intuitively. You tend to have a big heart, advocating for the underdog and may need more alone time than others. Though some may label you as needy or sensitive, your sensitivity is your strength.

Lesser Yin

The Lesser Yin is more flexible, with a composition that varies from 60 to 80 percent Yin energy and 20 to 40 percent Yang energy. You have a balanced nature, with a sensitivity and curiosity that fuels your creativity. While you may lean toward introversion and prefer going with the flow, you are self-aware and appreciate your unique journey of self-discovery. Though some may have a more dominant personality, you value your own process and are enthralled by the journey.

Lesser Yang

Now we are entering the realm of strong Yang/masculine energy (60 to 80 percent), which is more outgoing, dynamic, and assertive, often moving through life at a brisk pace. You possess a beautiful combination of open-mindedness, kindness, passion, and playfulness. You set high expectations for yourself but approach life with a healthy balance of creativity and practicality. A future-oriented mindset drives you, and you have a remarkable ability to achieve your goals while maintaining a positive outlook.

Greater Yang

Greater Yang energy is the epitome of masculinity. It is driven, focused on goals, accomplished, and dominant. This energy is associated with daytime, action, vision, and strength. You're a born leader with a natural ability to solve problems and make big things happen. Your drive and energy are undeniable, and you thrive on challenge and excitement. You've always known you were meant for great things, and you inspire others to follow in your footsteps.

ACTION STEPS

- Utilize visualization methods to imagine yourself in a state where the masculine and feminine energies within you are in equilibrium, creating balance and harmony.
- Develop self-awareness and introspection practices to better understand how your masculine and feminine energies influence your thoughts and behaviors.
- Nurture a mindset of appreciation and admiration for the masculine and feminine energies present in others, acknowledging that they are integral components of universal balance and harmony.
- Think of an area in your life you'd like to improve, like career or health. Then, create a plan to achieve that goal by breaking down the steps and making a timeline. Masculine energy is all about taking action and achieving goals.
- Pick one activity to cultivate feminine energy and include it in your daily or weekly routine. Begin with a few minutes a day and increase gradually. Be kind and patient with yourself as you explore this new aspect of yourself.

The Law of Gender is a powerful reminder that everyone possesses both feminine and masculine energies within them, regardless of their gender. The energies are complementary and necessary for manifestation, just like the Yin and Yang. This Law is not about conforming to traditional gender roles but finding a balance between the two energies. Masculine energy is the force of action, logic, and willpower, while feminine energy is the force of intuition, creativity, and empathy. Both energies are necessary to achieve a greater sense of wholeness and tap into our true potential.

The Law of Rhythm teaches us that all aspects of life, including the seasons, tides, and our emotional and personal cycles, follow a natural flow and cycle. Meanwhile, the Law of Gender reminds us to acknowledge and embrace the masculine and feminine energies within us, regardless of our gender identity. The link between these two Laws is that just as everything in life has its own rhythm and cycle, so do our expressions and embodiment of masculine and feminine energies. By honoring and accepting both energies within us, we can achieve balance and harmony in our lives.

Congratulations on reaching the end of this transformative book and embarking on a journey of self-discovery and manifestation through the Laws of the Universe. Through your understanding and knowledge of the 12 Universal Laws and how they operate in unison to create our world, you now have a powerful tool to manifest the life you desire. You can tap into the power of your thoughts, beliefs, and actions to align yourself with the energy of abundance, joy, and positivity. As you continue on this path, I have no doubt that you will manifest all you desire and live a life filled with love, purpose, and fulfillment. Keep shining your light and creating your reality, knowing that the Universe is always working in your favor. And with that, let's delve into our concluding thoughts.

Passing the Universal Torch

Armed with the insights of the 12 Universal Laws, it's now your moment to shine and guide others seeking the same enlightenment.

By sharing an honest review of this book on Amazon, you can point other seekers toward a reservoir of wisdom, ready to harness the Universal Laws to their advantage.

I appreciate your commitment. The Universe thrives when knowledge is shared, and you're playing a pivotal role in its ever-evolving dance.

CONCLUSION

The 12 Universal Laws are foundational principles that weave the intricate tapestry of existence and provide an understanding of the universe's rhythm and dynamics. Each law unravels a unique facet of our interaction with the cosmos. They teach us about our intrinsic interconnectedness, the formidable power of our thoughts and intentions, and the delicate balance that governs both the seen and unseen realms of existence. Let's briefly revisit their essence:

Law of Divine Oneness: Everything in the Universe is inter-connected. Our every thought, action, or event impacts the collective whole.

Law of Vibration: Everything has a unique vibrational frequency. By attuning our energies, we can influence our experiences and realities.

Law of Correspondence: Our outer world mirrors our inner world. By transforming our inner beliefs and feelings, we can reshape our external experiences.

Law of Attraction: We attract into our lives whatever we focus on, be it positive or negative.

Law of Inspired Action: Dreams and intentions are realized through inspired actions.

Law of Perpetual Transmutation of Energy: We have the power to change our circumstances by redirecting our energy and focus.

Law of Cause and Effect: Every action has an equivalent reaction, reminding us of the importance of responsibility and consciousness in our choices.

Law of Compensation: The Universe always compensates us for our deeds, ensuring that no good action goes unrewarded.

Law of Relativity: All experiences are subjective and can be transformed by changing our perspective.

Law of Polarity: Everything has an opposite, reminding us of the balance inherent in existence.

Law of Rhythm: Life has its ebbs and flows. By aligning with these natural rhythms, we can navigate our experiences more gracefully.

Law of Gender: Both masculine and feminine energies reside within us, and by harmonizing them, we find internal balance.

As you journeyed through this book, every chapter aimed to demystify a specific law, offering a blend of ancient wisdom and contemporary understanding. Beyond mere theory, these chapters were meticulously crafted to arm you with practical insights, actionable tools, and transformative exercises. This guide isn't just about comprehending the Universal Laws but also about integrating them into your daily life. By genuinely embracing and living in sync with these principles, you stand at a cosmic crossroad where every decision and intention aligns you with an endless reservoir of abundance, joy, and positivity.

Drawing from my personal narrative of overcoming challenges and rediscovering purpose, I can attest to the transformative might of these laws. They were the lighthouses that steered me away from stormy seas and towards a horizon of hope and fulfillment. This book is more than just pages of knowledge; it's a synthesis of lessons I've learned and the wisdom I'm eager to share. As you absorb and apply these teachings, I hope they serve as the wind beneath your wings, propelling you to soaring heights of self-discovery and realization.

Your journey with this book may have reached its conclusion, but the real adventure has only just begun. I invite you to reflect upon these teachings, apply them, and observe the subtle shifts in your life. And, if this guide has been a catalyst for change or provided you with newfound clarity, please share your experiences and feedback on Amazon. Your narrative might be the guiding star someone else is searching for.

In closing, remember that the path to manifesting your aspirations is paved with faith, perseverance, and continuous learning. While the Universal Laws offer profound insights, your personal experiences, reflections, and intuitions are equally essential. Trust the journey, cherish each moment, and know that with every step you take, the Universe conspires to support and uplift you. Namasté.

REFERENCES

Abundance No Limits. (n.d.). *The law of perpetual transmutation of energy mystery*. Abundance No Limits. Retrieved April 21, 2023, from https://www.abundancenolimits.com/law-of-perpetual-transmutation-of-energy/

Andary, C. (2021, May 25). *The law of cause and effect*. Create Good Karma This Way! LinkedIn. https://www.linkedin.com/pulse/law-cause-effect-create-good-karma-way-cheryl-andary-1c

Baskin-Sommers, A., Krusemark, E., & Ronningstam, E. (2014). Empathy in narcissistic personality disorder: From clinical and empirical perspectives. *Personality Disorders: Theory, Research, and Treatment, 5*(3). https://psycnet.apa.org/doiLanding?doi=10.1037%2Fper0000061

Blankert, T., & Hamstra, M. R. W. (2016). Imagining Success: Multiple Achievement Goals and the Effectiveness of Imagery. *Basic and Applied Social Psychology, 39*(1), 60–67. https://doi.org/10.1080/01973533.2016.1255947

Brown, B. (2021a, September 6). *Law of divine oneness | The 12 universal laws of manifestation*. Modern Manifestation. https://www.themodernmanifestation.com/post/law-of-divine-oneness

Brown, B. (2021b, September 20). *Law of vibration | The 12 universal laws of manifestation*. Modern Manifestation. https://www.themodernmanifestation.com/post/law-of-vibration

Brown, B. (2021c, October 18). *Law of correspondence | The 12 universal laws of manifestation*. Modern Manifestation. https://www.themodernmanifestation.com/post/law-of-correspondence

Brown, B. (2021d, November 15). *Law of cause and effect | The 12 universal laws of manifestation*. Modern Manifestation. https://www.themodernmanifestation.com/post/law-of-cause-and-effect

Brown, B. (2021e, December 27). *Law of perpetual transmutation of energy | The 12 universal laws of manifestation*. Modern Manifestation. https://www.themodernmanifestation.com/post/law-of-perpetual-transmutation-of-energy

Brown, B. (2022a, January 24). *Law of relativity | The 12 universal laws of mani-festation.* Modern Manifestation. https://www.themodernmanifestation. com/post/law-of-relativity

Brown, B. (2022b, March 14). *Law of gender | The 12 universal laws of manifesta-tion.* Modern Manifestation. https://www.themodernmanifestation.com/ post/law-of-gender

Chapman, C. (n.d.-a). *Create the life you want part 2: Apply law of correspondence.* Hearts Rise Up. Retrieved April 15, 2023, from https://heartsriseup.- com/create-the-life-you-want-part-2-apply-the-law-of-correspondence

Chapman, C. (n.d.-b). *Create the life you want part 5: Apply the law of rhythm.* Hearts Rise Up. Retrieved April 22, 2023, from https://heartsriseup.com/ create-the-life-you-want-part-5-apply-law-of-rhythm/

Cherry, K. (2022, October 11). *Why is it important to use empathy in certain situ-ations?* Verywell Mind. https://www.verywellmind.com/what-is-empathy- 2795562

Chikovani, G., Babuadze, L., Iashvili, N., Gvalia, T., & Surguladze, S. (2015). Empathy costs: Negative emotional bias in high empathisers. *Psychiatry Research, 229*(1-2), 340–346. https://doi.org/10.1016/j.psychres.2015. 07.001

Coster, D. (2019, January 21). *The law of polarity might change your life.* Psych Central. https://psychcentral.com/blog/the-law-of-polarity-might- change-your-life#2

Curran, D. (2021, June 17). *What is the law of perpetual transmutation of energy and how it works.* Our Subconscious Mind. https://oursubconsciousmind. com/what-is-the-law-of-perpetual-transmutation-of-energy-and-how-it- works/

Dandelion Training & Development. (2021, December 13). *The importance of gaining different perspectives.* Dandelion Training & Development. https:// dandeliontraininganddevelopment.com/2021/12/the-importance-of- perspective/

DiIorio, M. (2019a, January 5). *The law of cause and effect.* Wellismo. https:// www.wellismo.com/6-the-law-of-cause-and-effect/

DiIorio, M. (2019b, January 7). *The law of rhythm.* Wellismo. https://www. wellismo.com/11-the-law-of-rhythm/

Eastman, Q. (2013, December 2). *Mice can inherit learned sensitivity to a smell.* Emory University News Centre. https://news.emory.edu/stories/2013/ 12/smell_epigenetics_ressler/campus.html

Eatough, E. (2023, February 22). *What is the law of attraction and can you use it to change your life?* BetterUp. https://www.betterup.com/blog/what-is-law-of-attraction

Fox, M. (2022, August 31). *What is the law of cause and effect.* SelfMadeLadies. https://selfmadeladies.com/universal-laws-cause-effect/

Ganguly, I. (2020, February 17). *Law of vibration.* TheMindFool. https://themindfool.com/the-law-of-vibration/

Green, S. (2022, July 25). *4 ways to manifest success by using universal energy.* Success Consciousness. https://www.successconsciousness.com/blog/manifesting/manifest-success-using-universal-energy/

Hertz, C. (2022, January 29). *We are all connected through the law of divine oneness.* Living in the Glow. https://www.conniehertz.com/we-are-all-connected-through-the-law-of-divine-oneness/

Hillis, A. E. (2013). Inability to empathize: brain lesions that disrupt sharing and understanding another's emotions. *Brain, 137*(4), 981–997. https://doi.org/10.1093/brain/awt317

Hurst, K. (2016, August 22). *6 science facts that prove that the law of attraction exists.* The Law of Attraction. https://thelawofattraction.com/six-things-need-know-science-behind-law-attraction/

Hurst, K. (2021, July 28). *Universal energy: Be one with the universe's energy.* The Law of Attraction. https://thelawofattraction.com/universal-energy/

Jom, H. (2022, April 28). *How brain cells are like little universes.* The Epoch Times. https://www.theepochtimes.com/how-brain-cells-are-like-little-universes_334200.html

Jung, J. Y., Oh, Y. H., Oh, K. S., Suh, D. W., Shin, Y. C., & Kim, H. J. (2007). Positive-Thinking and Life Satisfaction amongst Koreans. *Yonsei Medical Journal, 48*(3), 371. https://doi.org/10.3349/ymj.2007.48.3.371

Keithley, Z. (2021, May 19). *What is inspired action? (A Manifestation Guide).* Zanna Keithley. https://zannakeithley.com/what-is-inspired-action-a-manifestation-guide/

Keithley, Z. (2022, June 6). *The law of polarity: What it is and why it matters.* Zanna Keithley. https://zannakeithley.com/law-of-polarity/

Keys Soulcare. (n.d.). *How to awaken your divine masculine energy.* Keys Soulcare. Retrieved April 22, 2023, from https://www.keyssoulcare.com/en_-CA/spirit/how-to-awaken-your-divine-masculine-energy.html#

Kimmes, J. G., & Durtschi, J. A. (2016). Forgiveness in Romantic Relationships: The Roles of Attachment, Empathy, and Attributions. *Journal of*

Marital and Family Therapy, 42(4), 645–658. https://doi.org/10.1111/jmft. 12171

Kuna, N. (n.d.). *The law of perpetual transmutation of energy.* Natalia Kuna. Retrieved April 21, 2023, from https://www.nataliakuna.com/the-law-of-perpetual-transmutation-of-energy.html

Lam, C. B., Solmeyer, A. R., & McHale, S. M. (2012). Sibling Relationships and Empathy Across the Transition to Adolescence. *Journal of youth and adolescence, 41*(12), 1657–1670. https://doi.org/10.1007/s10964-012-9781-8

LaMeaux, E. C. (n.d.). *How to attract good karma.* Gaiam. https://www.gaiam. com/blogs/discover/how-to-attract-good-karma

Lonnsburry, B. (2013, January 30). *The shocking truth about the law of attraction.* Live a Life You Love. https://livealifeyoulove.com/the-shocking-truth-about-the-law-of-attraction/

Lotzof, K. (2018). *Are we really made of stardust?* Natural History Museum. https://www.nhm.ac.uk/discover/are-we-really-made-of-stardust.html

Louise, E. (2022, March 23). *How to take inspired action to manifest with the law of attraction.* Through the Phases. https://www.throughthephases.com/inspired-action-manifestation/

Manasa. (2021, October 9). *Law of compensation: Ultimate law of universe For success.* Wealthful Mind. https://wealthfulmind.com/law-of-compensation-law-universe-for-success/

Meloy, R. S. (2019, April 24). *Balancing our feminine and masculine energy.* Pause Meditation. https://www.pausemeditation.org/single-post/balancing-feminine-masculine-energy

Motley, B. (2021a). *The spiritual meanings of numbers.* Self-published.

Motley, B. (2021b). *From the universe with love.* Spiritual Growth.

Nintem, Z. (2018a, March 27). *Universal law: Law of gender.* Higher Vibes Life. http://www.highervibeslife.com/universal-law-law-of-gender/

Nintem, Z. (2018b, March 27). *Universal law: Law of rhythm.* Higher Vibes Life. http://www.highervibeslife.com/universal-law-law-of-rhythm/

Nintem, Z. (2021, April 23). *Universal law: Law of relativity.* The Fearless Hustle. https://thefearlesshustle.com/universal-law-law-of-relativity/

Nolan, C. (Director). (2015). *Interstellar* [Film]. Legendary Pictures; Syncopy; Lynda Obst Productions.

Nuur, D. (2018, July 19). *Masculine and feminine energy - balancing masculine & feminine.* Goop. https://goop.com/wellness/spirituality/balancing-your-feminine-and-masculine-energies/

Oberlin, K. (2017, October 5). *As within so without, as above so below.* Holistic Connections. https://holistic-connections.net/2017/10/05/as-within-so-without-as-above-so-below/

Open College. (n.d.). *Law of cause and effect, cosmic law of action, karmic ripples.* Open College. https://www.opencollege.info/law-of-cause-and-effect/

A quote by C.G. Jung. (n.d.). Goodreads. https://www.goodreads.com/quotes/tag/polarity

A quote by Jim Carrey. (n.d.). Goodreads. https://www.goodreads.com/quotes/1259043-as-far-as-i-can-tell-it-s-just-about-letting

A quote by Laurie Perez. (n.d.). Goodreads. https://www.goodreads.com/quotes/tag/transmutation

A quote by Marcus Aurelius. (n.d.). Medium. https://medium.com/illumination/use-the-law-of-relativity-to-change-your-thinking-and-improve-your-life-45fc5ffab516

A quote by Margaret Fuller. (n.d.). Goodreads. https://www.goodreads.com/quotes/788192-male-and-female-represent-the-two-sides-of-the-great

A quote by Marianne Williamson. (n.d.). Goodreads. https://www.goodreads.com/work/quotes/21548696-the-law-of-divine-compensation

A quote by Nanette Mathews. (n.d.). Goodreads. https://www.goodreads.com/quotes/8450054-manifestation-without-action-is-only-a-wish

A quote by Nikola Tesla. (n.d.). Goodreads. https://www.goodreads.com/quotes/361785-if-you-want-to-find-the-secrets-of-the-universe

A quote by Oprah Winfrey. (n.d.). Goodreads. https://www.goodreads.com/quotes/48624-you-get-in-life-what-you-have-the-courage-to

A quote by Ralph Waldo Emerson. (n.d.). Goodreads. https://www.goodreads.com/quotes/57008-shallow-men-believe-in-luck-or-in-circumstance-strong-men

A quote by Rumi. (n.d.). The Wisdom Post. https://www.thewisdompost.com/self-improvement/thought/seek-seeking-rumi/2611

A quote by Swami Vivekananda. (n.d.). Goodreads. https://www.goodreads.com/quotes/178989-all-differences-in-this-world-are-of-degree-and-not

A Quote by Three Initiates. (n.d.). Goodreads. https://www.goodreads.com/author/quotes/30372.Three_Initiates

A quote by Unknown. (n.d.). Wikipedia. https://en.wikipedia.org/wiki/As_Above

Regan, S. (2021, June 17). *You've heard of the law of attraction — but how about the*

law of vibration? Mindbodygreen. https://www.mindbodygreen.com/arti
cles/law-of-vibration

Rotar, S. (2022, December 3). *The true spiritual meaning of the universe.* Mental
Style Project. https://mentalstyleproject.com/spiritual-meaning-of-the-
universe/

Santilli, M. (2022, April 22). *Why is everyone obsessed with manifesting and does it
actually work?* SELF. https://www.self.com/story/does-manifesting-work

Shamay-Tsoory, S. G., Aharon-Peretz, J., & Perry, D. (2009). Two systems for
empathy: a double dissociation between emotional and cognitive empathy
in inferior frontal gyrus versus ventromedial prefrontal lesions. *Brain,
132*(3), 617–627. https://doi.org/10.1093/brain/awn279

Sholer, A. (2017). *LoA lingo: A glossary of law of attraction phrases and terms.* Real
Life Law of Attraction. https://www.real-life-law-of-attraction.com/
lingo.html

Singal, V. (2020, June 22). *Karma - The law of cause and effect.* The Pioneer.
https://www.dailypioneer.com/2020/state-editions/karma---the-law-of-
cause-and-effect.html

Singh, A. A. (2020, October 13). *Council post: The mystery and science behind the
law of attraction.* Forbes. https://www.forbes.com/sites/forbescoachescoun
cil/2020/10/13/the-mystery-and-science-behind-the-law-of-attraction/?
sh=220708cf1a55

Tolle, E. (2016). *The power of now : a guide to spiritual enlightenment.* Yellow Kite.

Vilhauer, J. (2020, July 27). *How your thinking creates your reality.* Psychology
Today. https://www.psychologytoday.com/us/blog/living-forward/
202009/how-your-thinking-creates-your-reality

Wanderlust Worker. (2019). *5 reasons why everything happens for a reason in life.*
Wanderlust Worker. https://www.wanderlustworker.com/5-reasons-
why-everything-happens-for-a-reason-in-life/

Wang, Y. (2016, October 5). *Between humans and the universe: All we have are the
connections we make.* Situation Critical Fall 2016. https://sites.northwest
ern.edu/situationcritical/2016/10/05/between-the-universe-and-
humans-all-we-have-are-the-connections-we-make/

Whitman, C. (2022, February 25). *What synchronicities mean (and no, they're not
just coincidences).* YourTango. https://www.yourtango.com/experts/
christy-whitman/what-are-synchronicities-synchronicity-examples

Wong, K. (2021, April 24). *The spiritual meaning of the universe.* The Millennial

Grind. https://millennial-grind.com/the-spiritual-meaning-of-the-universe/